NK

An Artist JOURNEY

Author
POOJA KUMBHAR

NK

An artist journey

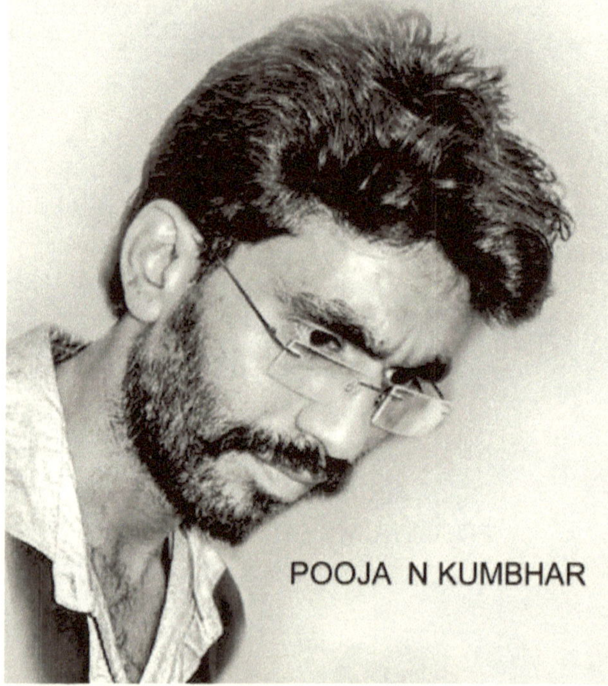

POOJA N KUMBHAR

DEDICATED TO

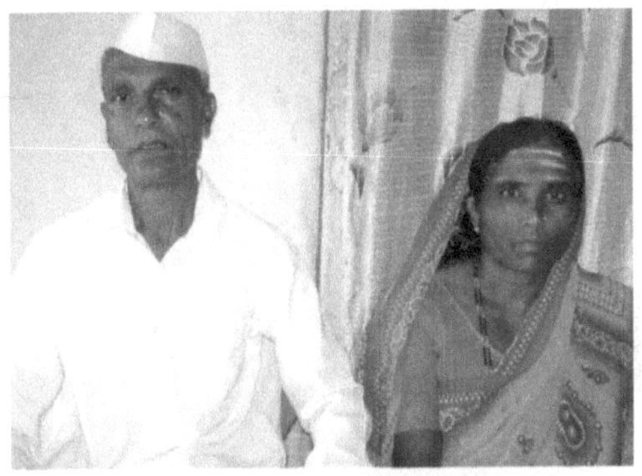

ARTIST NAGRAJ FATHER
SHRI REVANSIDDA AND MOTHER IRAMMA

NK an artist biography

Contents:

Acknowledgements
Foreword
Preface
HEARTFELT SPEECH BY RAMESH JOSHI
INTRODUCTION
BIRTH AND CHILDHOOD
NAGRAJ IS AN ARTIST OF INTERNATIONAL FAME
ABOUT PAINTING WORK
ART CAMPS AND WORKSHOP
NATIONAL AND INTERNATIONAL ART SOLO EXHIBITION
GROUP EXHIBITION IN NATIONAL
AWARDS AND FELICITION
OPINION OF LEGENDRY PEOPLE
LITERATURE JOURNEY
JOURNEY OF FILM WORLD
ARTICLES WRITTEN BY REPORTERS-
LETTERS FROM LEGENDRY ARTISTS
MEMORY WITH GREAT WRITERS COLLECTION
WITH LEGEDND ARTIST MEMORY PHOTOES
ARTIST PAINTING AND DRAWING COLLECTION
PUBLISHED PAPER CUTTING COLLECTION and media
OPINAN
BIO-DATA

AcKnowledgements

NK An artist biography WRITTEN
 BY POOJA NAGRAJ KUMBHAR
Mail-NagrajKumbhar@gmail.com
1st edition-2023
Copy right-Authors
Pages-121
Cover design- artist Nagraj
Author-Pooja Nagraj
Typing-Kumbhar prakashan

FOREWORD

My well wishers, reader, and family as well as book lovers...NK an life journey of Nagraj Kumbhar....comes to us and you will definitely like it...whatever success you get in life is your inspiration and I wish that I need your love more than your sympathy..i hope your love will remain like this for me.

Many through my writing I want to get a chance to win many hearts today.again I express sincere gratitude to those who helped me to write this and gave guidance to me.i got inspiration to write this book from Nagraj, due to impressions of his achievements in artistic world ...I am deeply grateful to him...

To reach the pinnacle of success not only flower is important but a bud a flower is also important...everyone's help is a need for success because we can't achieve our goal without any one's support..This book is dedicated to Nagraj Kumbhar and in this book shows black and white shades of his life journey ...

NK an artist biography

PREFACE

This story contains life journey of Nagraj Kumbhar ,I am writing this documentary to show the some of achievements of famous author Nagraj Kumbhar.he has versatile personality he is well known writer,he has written so many books ,he is achieved in several fields like drama,artist,director,in film industry,as a painter,as a photography and he worked as a humble teacher ..His achievement and awards from different states, exhibitions, totally life journey of Nagraj Kumbhar all over india that inspired me to write this book..the purpose of this story is to bring abilities in young children and hope to many other artists.this story gives inspiration to many people .i wrote this story based on reference of Nagraj Kumbhar ,I seen this person very closely ,this documentary reveals information about life journey of NK. to write this it takes me more than six months.

One artist after getting success everyone praise him and recognize him but when he grew in success path he faced so many obstacles,deficiencies,in that situation no one come infront to recognize..If we give little motivation by recognizing them they will grow and get success in short time...So many artists waiting to out his talent, to show their talent to world but they are lack of motivation and they leading their life unknowingly.

I respectfully request godfathers, artist world and everyone to motivate artists, praise them, give them help to come up of their world and show their talent to world.Nagraj Kumbhar well known, talented but once in a while he didn't have food to eat, he is suffering problems in his life .he worked hard and moved up and come up with the poor situation and now he is recognized as international artist

- **Pooja N Kumbhar**

HEARTFELT SPEECH BY RAMESH JOSHI

This life is like this only, it is impossible to say when and what time who will be introduced by whom...That' how the painter Nagraj Kumbhar introduced by narayan Joshi...on this occasion,when all his friends came together to establish a cultural association ,he introduced me as music director ...in the meeting I presented the idea that situation of artists don't have money or financial problem that's why Nagraj agreed when told that if we held a concert that the "water for the lake will be spilled into the lake "it will help our association financially...other member wondered if they should grow by themselves .i told them to give eight days time,this is not possible for them ,I will do it and show them ...then may be Nagraj seems to see something in me ..a few days ahead in aradhana school they invited me to school anniversary and they impressed by my kishorekumar songs...he wondered by seeing this boy .both of our thoughts came together ..Next when I know the composition for songs...immediately he said I will write ten songs and you give the lyrics composition ...they released "haadu nammadu dhwani nimmadu"audio albums .upcoming days our friendship grow more deeper and deeper...its bewilderment when he says me that sir I will write a book based on your life knowing all the dimensions of yourself..I said the book of possessions of persons have fallen into one corner center, its became funny...our disputes with them continued for one year...Finally they conveyed me..he said that he will make a documentary film like that....while giving shocks to one another he has written a book titled "the most brilliant artist "and is seen as an author and publisher...after the release of my film "nadapriyana nadayana short film .which I had been waiting for, I saw a very talented director ...our friendship with Nagraj Kumbhar a thoughtful artist of new new dimensions started from 2014 and we

NK an artist biography

have not only become friends but also brothers ..They called me to banglore for programme....they introduced me to many artists …sir Nagraj Kumbhar multilingual poet, director and painter …

Many of my stories have been directed into short films and introduced on social media…he acted in many films as a good actor .many more films are In the pipeline .he got many national and international awards ..In cinema he has bright future with this his life partner pooja stands as an inspiration and backbone to him...God gives this family to wealth, longlife and be protected …

Sri Nagraj Kumbhar founder of "NK ART AND FILMS" and I pray to god should keep going in his field...We are lucky to have such a versatile talented artist with us

- Ramesh Joshi
Singer and music composer,
Kalaburgi

CHAPTER-1
INTRODUCTION

India got independence in 1947 but Hyderabad –conotic kingdom was still under king-maharaja.it was in Hyderabad nizam administration in the year 1948 karnataka .the nizam was freed from the tyranny of the government and all the villages in the region became independent of the nizam administration .some of the farmers themselves began to cultivate some of the land .some farmers toiled at the headman of village.   economically backward farmers leaving their villages and wandering places and there was a flood of drought everywhere. Farmers' lives were in crisis .It has also become very difficult to get grains ,people have lost their lives and animals ..Many were sold gone .....

Nagraj grand father rudrappa and grandmother siddamma lived in heroor (b) village...Rudrappa and siddamma had two sons shankarappa and revanasiddappa...After the death of their parents shankarappa and revansiddappa grown in tha hands of ratnamma, ratnamma had taken the responsibility of these two sons..   And married these sons to a well family…shankrappa expired later due to back injury…revansidda became orphan and he got married to iramma….they have three sons and one daughter…siddram, shrishail and Nagraj and rajeshwari...

CHAPTER-2

BIRTH AND CHILDHOOD:

Nagaraj revanasiddha Kumbhar from Gulbarga, Born in a heroor-(B)Village of Gulbarga district on march 3,1987, who grew up in Maharashtra,he is the youngest son to his father... built up a strong sense that art should be made from raw things at home and the world should become natural raw material for art.

his father was born as a young son to his parents...dad left the state to live in ashtvinayaka sri kshetra ozar, Maharashtra, nagaraj was taken to primary school, where he didn't know a word of Marathi .his guruji bhaskar kaude changed name nagappa to Nagraj, and went school without a pen, pencil or book .since then he started Marathi medium and studied till puc...

When he was a little boy,in school days he did not have drawing materials because of shortage of money .four years of his childhood he couldn't get materials to draw but he was very interested in painting, by seeing interest of his artwork, madam had to brought him materials....he found himself a solution for drawing papers... when In school students from highschool throwing note page round balls from window,Nagraj collected those round pages and he made a book from those papers and made draw in them...he used to prepare colour from plants and craft materials from waste materials in home during the school holidays..he was interested in film ,drama,acting and dance since from childhood,he was impressed by bollywood actor akshay kumar,madhuri dixit,ajay devgan and amitabh bacchan ,often he collected hero and heroine pics ..He had a dream of becoming actor...after primary he joined to highschool he got a good art teacher vasant phule and B R dumbre sir and got guidance of art from these teachers ...he did not get uniform In school days because of general cost that time, to get uniform he worked as waiter in hotel And purchased himself uniform..

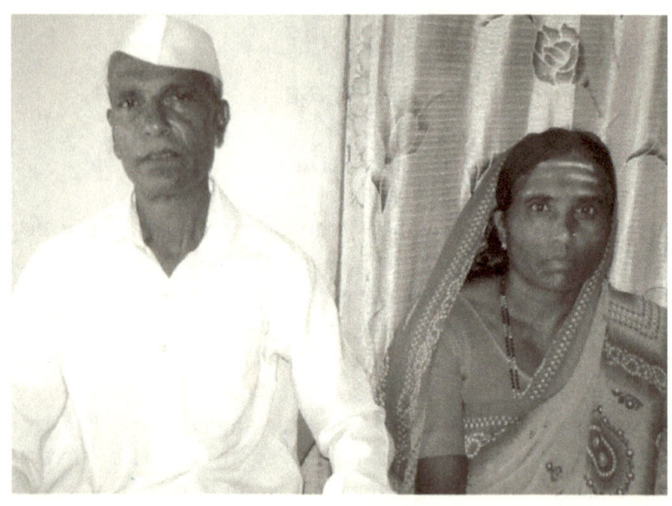

ARTIST NAGRAJ FATHER REVANSIDDA AND MOTHER IRAMMA

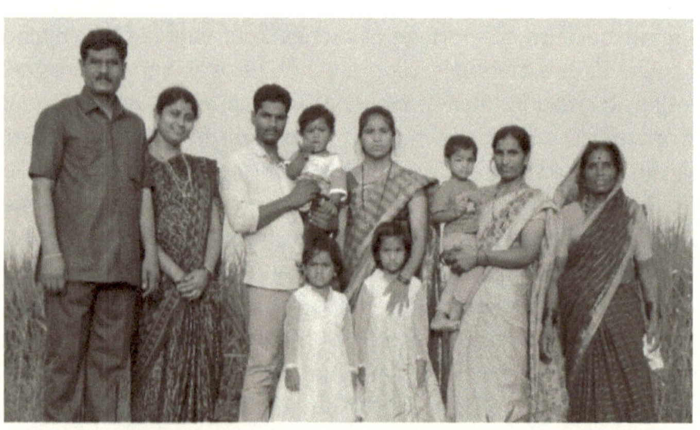

FAMILY OF NAGRAJ KUMBHAR WITH BROTHERS AND SISTER

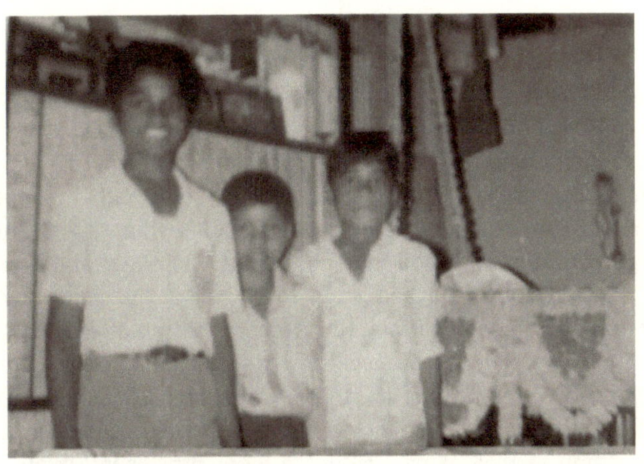

NAGRAJ AND HIS BROTHER IN CHILDHOOD

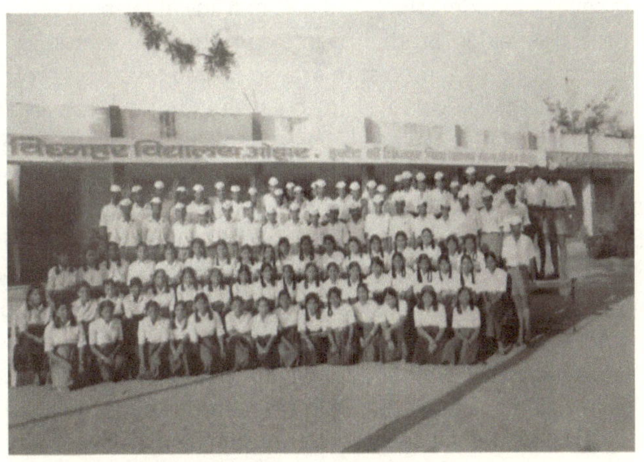

School group in pune Maharashtra

He   participated in the painting competition organized by the school and got a prize and when he needed more money, in holidays he went to the work of a constructing   building and earn money and from that money he took the study materials for future high Education and collected regional funds for the competition and when he was in seventh standard he got the state camel award for the painting, this painting competition organized by Marathi sakala news paper.. This is the time first he got his name in Marathi newspaper during his school days. As well as he got best honest monitor award at tenth standard. Spotty people appreciated him in front of his father and mother because of his good achievement, hard work, and honesty...He became the reason for his father, mother's happiness...Art teacher phule sir suggested to the Nagraj after Pu college education that you should join Fine Art College and become a great artist in art field and told to Nagraj if you want any help definitely will support you...you remember me.after the school education he joined pu college Ra pa subnis vidya mandir narayangaon.. during puc in college days he participated in many competitions like singing,dancing ,poem writing and drawing painting competition as well as he written so many articles in Marathi news papers as like lokmat,yuva sakal,tarun bharat,sanchar and in some magazines ..After completing puc college in Maharashtra he searched fine art college for admission, he didn't had any idea about art college that time...His elder brother wants him to join in science field department bt he had interest in art...so he requested his brother to join in art college...Because of his creativity and interests in art his brother joined him to Gulbarga fine art college in 2003... the MMK college of visual art is one of famous college in Gulbarga under the guidance of artist V G ANDANI..He struggled in his college life because of his poor situation...He recently migrated from pune, Maharashtra to Karnataka, pleasant to join college in own motherland (kalburgi)...His elder brother siddaram recently joined in police department of Karnataka ...and he get three thousand salary per month... And he pay thousand rupees to Nagraj for his art education and he has to manage all the art sources for his education, painting material...Nagraj and his second elder brother shrishail both are living together in rented room in Gulbarga.both brothers studying in Gulbarga, both brothers are dependent on their elder brother siddaram, because of his minimum salary he couldn't pay for the both education..Sometimes he struggling for his life to manage his own basic needs... after the college time he was going to bus stand, railway station as welll as outdoor land scapes for practice , during college time he did many landscapes and sketches...sometimes he earned from portrait of some people as welll as leaders.. He worked hard in painting by day and night in college...He spent more time in his art work only.. Got more encouragement with the support of his mother and father and the guidance of art gurus,his brother was very nervous when he spend more money and more time in art education because he known about this art field that there is no end and no guarantee for successful life ,that was very challenging task for Nagraj ,but he didn't lose hope ,he believed in god and in his own work..After five years of hard work his first painting were sold at five thousand rupees in his student life. That was very emotional and it was first step and first hope to success life … after the completion of BFA,he continued his post graduation in master of visual arts .he got HRD scholarship from ministry of culture at new delhi at 2011.. He did external hard work himself acrylic media on canvas more than thirty paintings...he achieved in art and got several awards...He organized his first solo exhibition successfully in kerala..

MFA finished without further he joined sriguru vidya Mandir College, raichur as a Guest lecture and mentored thousands of painter students and went to Hampi University as an evaluator and gained experience During his graduation, personally participated in various art competitions and won prizes and also participated in structured art camps and participated in the gathering as journalist.

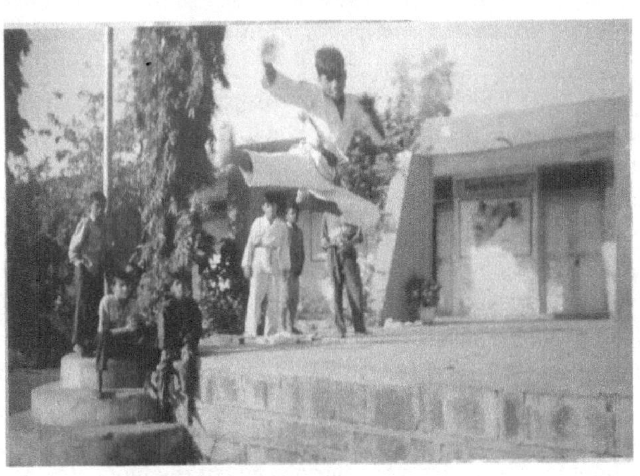

NAGRAJ KUMBHAR IMRESSED BY AKSHYKUMAR

NK an artist biography

ACTION FILMS FROM CHILDHOOD

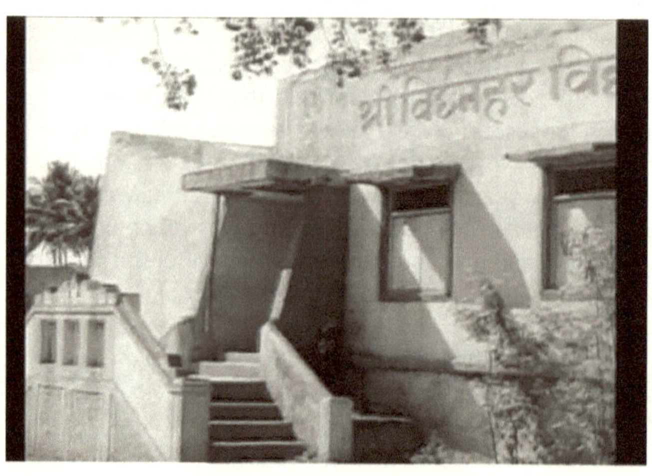

Shri vighnahar vidhyalay ozar school pune

He also started writing art criticism articles in many news papers and wrote many columns...He has won 2011 rajyotsava in painting award from Gulbarga University, pratibha kala award from university pratibhotsava, yogadana tilak award from pune, all these awards at young age...

At this age, more than 100 paintings have come to various districts of the country; winning award for art exhibitions and even there his art has been recognized and encouraged.

Nagaraj is grateful because many works of art have been sold .His art exhibitions have been presented in places like Karnataka,delhi,Chandigarh,Mumbai,Hyderabad,mysore,

lucknow,uttarpradesh etc Artist Nagraja's paintings are on display at naganhalli police training centre, MMK art school, vijaya hagargundgi museum gallery in Gulbarga and his paintings are sold in Germany, Australia, and in India.

These are not just aristic pictures but also emotional pictures of some famous people among them the famous guy of the hindi film industry madhuri dixit, freedom fighter vidyadhar guruji, famous literary vasant kushtagi international artist pro V.G Andani's portrait

NK an artist biography

flourished from his hands .At a very young age he traveled around different parts of the country.realized his dream, and wish him to bring the richness of the art....

he has innovated by writing in Kannada .there is no language barrier for talent .on the way of life, he started the adventure of writing an article, writing poetry with he wrote about his own village story and developed an intrest in their god, belief, and culture and becoming better to know about their village to the world. Nagraj Kumbhar is a young artist developed a passion for painting in his childhood .the teachers cheered. Artist from foreign states who have made this way of life are inviting him and allowing him to exhibit his paintings .but he is not satisfied with this .he want to exhibit his paintings internationally .he worked hard for it. Art should flourish from the raw materials available at home .nagaraj revanasidda was a famous potter from Gulbarga who grew up in poverty with a very dream of becoming an artist for the world.He was born as the last son and lived a life of poverty in the hope of his parents.

Second national student workshop 2008 mysore,gangavati youth festival 2008,moodbidri alvas varnajagrati competition 2010, 2005-2006 recently MMK animation camp ,terrakotta,portrait ,graphic, mural (cement) various artistic competitions and workshops organized in the institute Merit scholarship in 2007 for awards and scholarship First prize and gold medal,silver medal in youth festival at gangavati in 2008. Merit scholarships in 2009-2010 scholarship, 2010 kala mahotsava painting award Kava college mysore art gallery 2008 and performance award .2005-2006 to present line... it is not to continuoue to conduct various exhibitions every year in an institute which is being educated till now.. In 2008 ,lalitha kala academy,lokamanya tilak exhibition poona , painting exhibition in 2009 banglore,mini kala exhibition in Hyderabad ,primer talent exhibition in manglore,festival art exhibition in bidar .ujjaini madhyapradesh selected for artist conference ...Presently in the year 2010-11 kochi has been selected for the gallery's art...this art painting is not a learned skill ,it must have come as a gift from god.

it is only possible when the story is always faithfully tried...it is a skill of highlight the reality when a scene first catches the eye and it is perceived in the mind.. It requires concentration, skill and perfection

.thus the artist is emotional in his own right However, their art become worthwhile when they amuse people and get recognition from them. Conduct few shows and   preparing for the next...

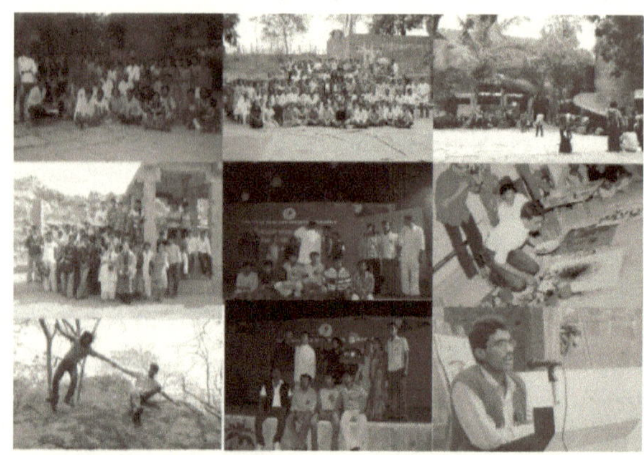

ART EDUCATION IN FINE ART COÏLEGE GULBARGA

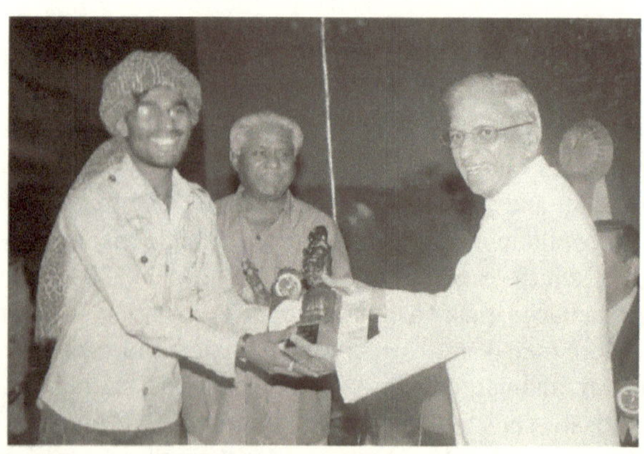

AWARDED BY FORMER SUPREME COURT JUDGE SHIVRAJ PATIL

CHAPTER-3
ABOUT PAINTING WORK

Young Nagraj kumbar's hold a master of visual artist from Gulbarga university, he has actively participated In several camps and National level exhibition during the last 30 years from his academic carrier.. He always have a almost strong kind of desires about Indian contemporary.. few of listed art activities phenomenon..

Therefore Nagraj continuously unfolded with his strong space of memory to unlimited real kind of contemporary a true aesthetics kind of art conscience such act by Nagraj's presented some assonant author different kind of art viewers.he offers through his works to such lyrically some kind of art caretakers and humbly hunter's for very exotic kind of visual worlds,rarely existed in scripture ordinance instanced craze of like made by the past history's ancient art form of these such civilization .it appears like that great earliest period most globalized civilization .for instance "unending hamlet" the title of these attested work summons up in one's mind a graveyard like space ,but is a reference really tro the dwelling into was these as well bread most Indian tiny hamlet .thpough the Nagraj's work of art that depicted some persist on elucidate to the elude Here images or forms both seems prima facie like a aviary or some north Indian rural usage for their daily basic food preparartion bake bale although looking like Indian roman "amphitheatre" but when we try to find that onto logical meaning is vey clearly tell us about north Karnataka tiny hamlet song of phraseology is constructed sensuously such sentence of very antiqualed trough .this overall of drama include one clearly highlighted yoga posed and bended surreal vessel of tea embodied figure atop try to tell us something about the sacred eco system story with spitting these balanced liliputian window's little bit of smokes Another one Nagraj's work here" towards the enlightment "the title of the work will be very clearly appears ...it purely seeming's with strtokes of bold and forced abstract kind of element overall ..but we try to look in depth of these theme will be including more types of things right and left sides.these in movement a plastic cups of elemented multitude will be attempt for meticulous observation to themselves by bus from this centered situated big pallor of multiplic and mystic mum

Now we are talking Nagraj concept a north karnataka's most having in most villages stone carving elevated ancient asset's of the chalukya dynasty made more shivalinga temples with he lobby having a two left and right side of beautiful carving dwarpalaka's these all temples have in front of their this ladder kind of ancient lights arranging popular formation of pillar .through this great traditional pillar Nagraj try to tell as about a secret story nothing happens enlightment a without having cuktural cultivation in us this is very universal key to must understanding of everyone

Here another one Nagraj's title of the work "grievance amidst living " a clearly picturized In this form of early styled borewell shape is carved with some of very mind blossoming visualization .the springe is overall cap a pie contained with deeply voluminous insight witch is put bold question to infront of the intellectual viewers was stepled in side that pictorial mastrix enclosed with maladyness human filed looking like man hole cabin kind of vision looks sharply such inseration comprehensive lines within that ,maestro depiction.
 what agenda is riding trough that play full pictures stipulated about a having complicity of careveer because of needed or regard sufficient resources is today not available to enough level.so that today's man kind will be living into that in habit
Of deficiency life which this our current globe having, mass of overloaded maximum globally growed population .journey of
life ,with stark staped typed fill in at stake pictures tells story with balancely dangling stair's generation in the few corner with a megre generation most of percentage contented clearly with grievance of food water extra what really for basic needed resourse for balanced livelihoods instead there is a having immesurable ,here Nagraj put a meekly massage about this suffering for living life ,of a

merge worlds population picture into that membrance scarcity of
the life scenario
Often here one or some coincidences happens with Nagraj thoughts
simultaneously that matter is icon able to understand form my level
of general knowledge   indirectly his   sunconcious pulsating   with
some recent   occurred "subgeographical wonders " of under water
dictation … recently into this globe one report has come out in this
year science and vast technology is a now

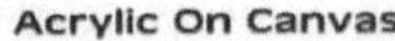

Acrylic On Canvas

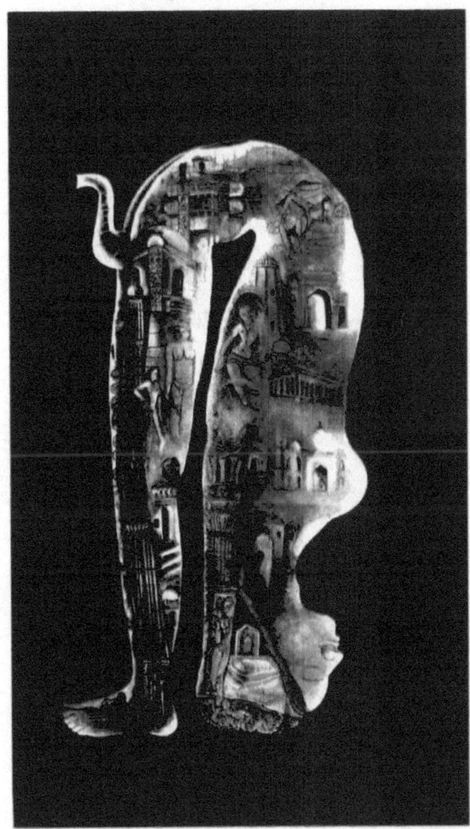

Journy 2   **84"x48"**

find out   certainly comprehensive chanel of under water chest gigantic circulation of underwater what our savior was already made for our globe to take care of protection itself.Its might Nagraj's visual story telling is forever have some meaning full exploring forms and different typed substanitial stenography of his works .... These forms and artefacts leads as enter into vivid imaginative worlds, although that was one of our cosmos true scenario .the contemporaneous practice of imbalancing of eco system   intensity of perceptions are also evident .and also Nagraj was one of distinctive evidence for his sensation male and female both the younger artists whose come to this field be came a serious visual artist....

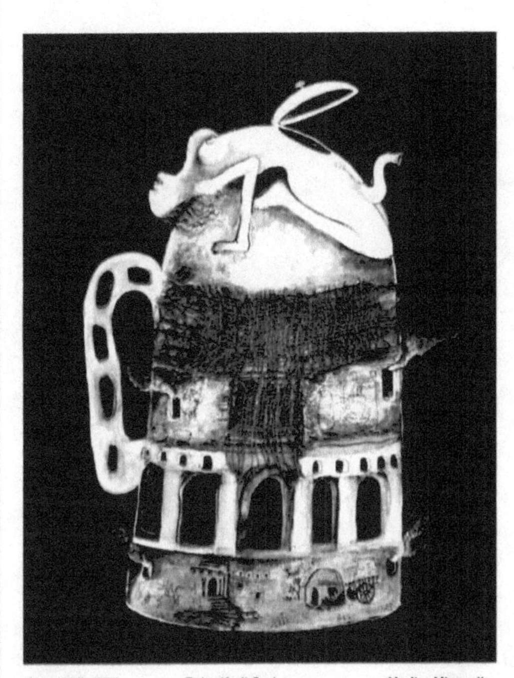

Size: 30"x 22"   Title: Ketli Series   Media: Mixmedia

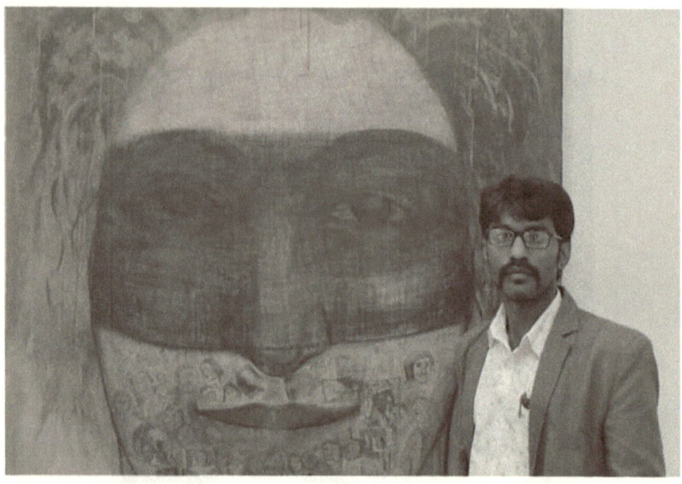

Creativity and creation

The recent work of a young artist form Karnataka,Nagraj Kumbhar in acrylic colours on canavas is simply awesome and astonishing .it shows his deep obsession with nature and its vivid marvels in a very district and lucrative visual forms.. that are not only thematic ,innovative   but also lyrical deeply influenced by nature and it's wonders   since childhood,Nagraj decided to put   his childhood memories and life experiences like struggle keen ambitions and hardships   as well as agony and sufferings etc on canvas ..he decided   to   express   his   vivid   impressions   about enjoyment,enlightment and visual panorama of various aranas in nature and their deep impaction human mind ... due to this ,his works are endowed with good aesthetic value and nice total rhythemic of colours which are truly distinct and unique ... His work , "towards   the enlightment " shows   the deep   reverence   and gratitude for the pleasure one gets due to excellence in arts like ,singing, performing etc ..the works showing nature and its vivid visual forms illustrate the rhythm of life through seasonal highlights of flower, petals, fruits, etc and the   ardent human   desire to achieve these pleasures as well as the materialistic ones through sustained effort and preservance ..his works on " human face " revealing an amalgamation of different feelings inside the sensitive mind certainly provides the relevant visual joy and exhilarations to all…

In a way ,Nagraj Kumbhar has adorned his latest series with in innovative ideas and tonal rhythm of colours but with a realistic attitude towards life as well as clarity of the artistic expression there in.

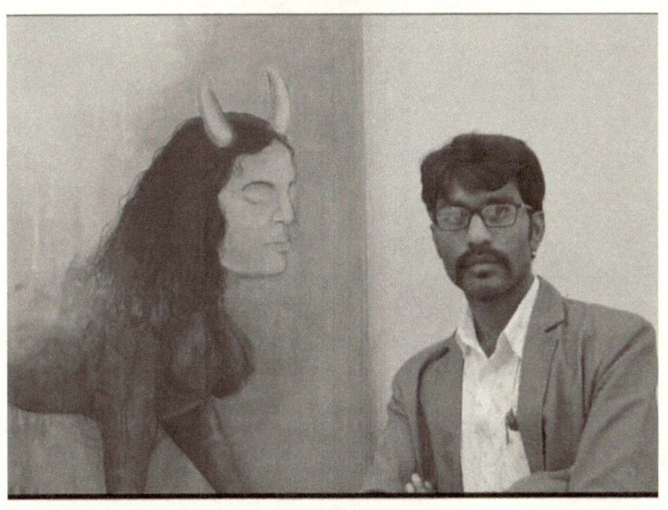

ARTIST NAGRAJ WITH NATIONAL PAINTING AWARDEE

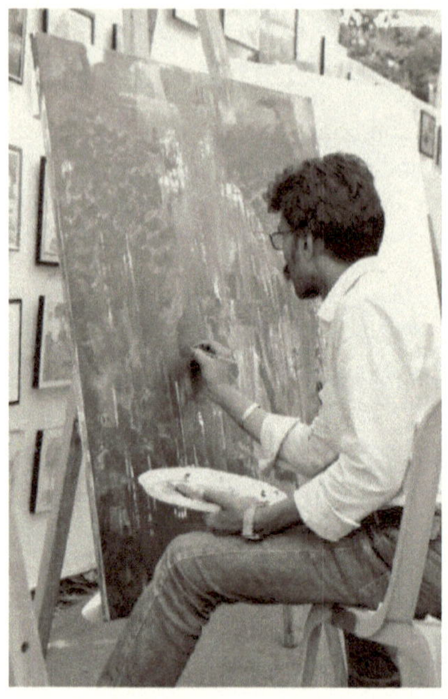

ARTIST NAGRAJ PAINTING DEMO IN NATIONAL CAMP ODISSA

this presentation being very distant and transparent as well as tonally clear truly renders ample visual pleasure and mental relaxation   to all common   viewers as   well as   art patrons/connoisseurs leading   to their   warm   response and appreciation that will Truly inspire and encourage him for his forthcoming artistic presentations in the future endeavours…

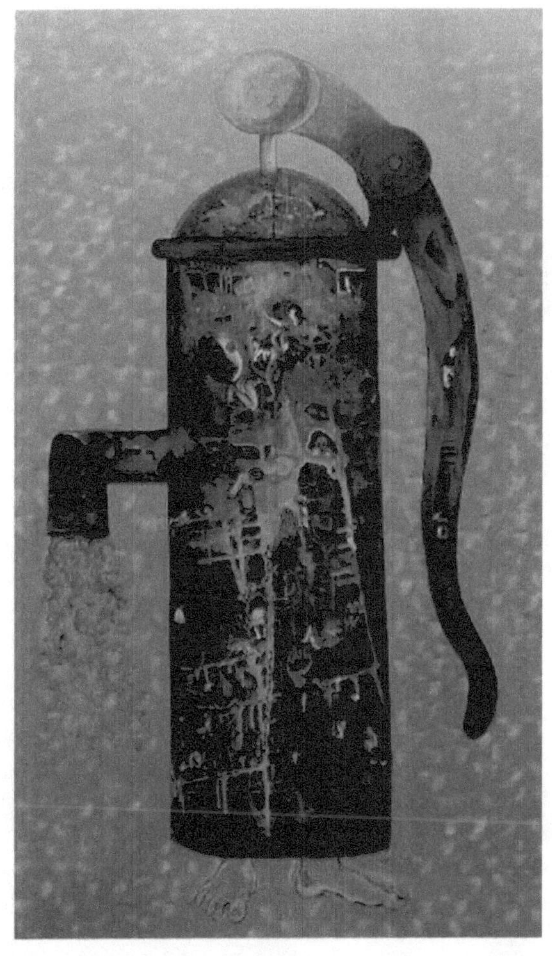

ACRYLIC ON CANVAS 'HUMAN SESTOM' SIZE 48X84 IN

CHAPTER-4
ART CAMPS AND WORKSHOP

2010: Alva's Varna jagruti state art camp in mood bidri
2010: kalaparva (Ujjain) student artist camp in the international,2013: the voice of canvas "artist camp organized by Orissa modern art gallery in bhuvaneshwar ,Orissa state 2013:artist camp april 15'the world art day'artist camp in Gulbarga, 2013:all india artist camp the "doon valley public "deoband ,sarangapur (up)2015: national art camp"kirti "ebes engineering College, gaziabad Delhi ,2015: Gulbarga artist camp in Gulbarga, by Gulbarga academy of fine art, Gulbarga

ART WORKSHOP:
2005,2005,2006,2006,2007,2007:animation   camp,terracotta camp,portrait camp, sculpture camp, traditional camp ,calligraphy held in MMK college of visual art Gulbarga 2008:2nd national art student workshop CAVA College Mysore 2009,2009:graphic workshop, mural camp,in cement,MMK college of visual art ,2010: creative design workshop MMK College of visual art Gulbarga...
PARTICIPATION ART COMPETATION
2008: youth festival gangavati, 2008:22nd lokamanya tilak arts, exhibition pune, 2008: lalit kala academy Selection, 38th annual art exhibition manglore, 2009: primer talent league art Exhibition, manglore, 2009: Gulbarga university Gulbarga pratibha mahotsav art exhibition Gulbarga, 2009:23rdlokamanya tilak art exhibition pune, 2009: art and culture national exhibition Gulbarga 2009: bidar festival art exhibition...2010: Pratibha yuva mahotsav art exhibition, 2010: Gulbarga university Gulbarga, inter college competition, 2010: kampu painting exhibition In Gulbarga, 2012:25th silver jubilee lokmanya tilak art exhibition pune,2012: group photograph exhibition held in chaitanmayi art gallery Gulbarga...
 KUMBH KALA KENDRA, ART ACTIVITY
A Two days national painting camp organized by the kumbh kala Kendra recently in Gulbarga.the camp was held from Oct 2-10 in the city...

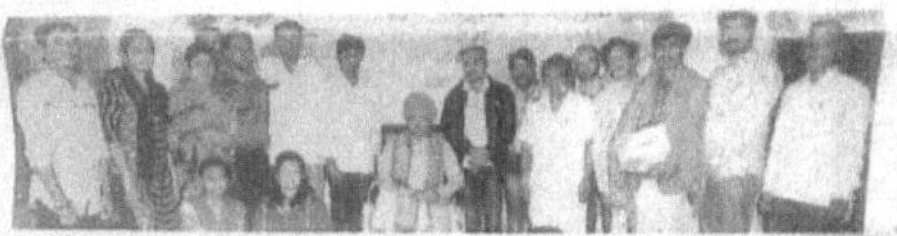

National art camp at in Gulbarga

A two days National painting camp organized by the Kumbh Kala Kendra concluded recently in Gulbarga. The camp was held from October 2-10 in the city. The paintings were created on the life an incident of Poojya Shri Channaveer Shivayogi of Babaladi Math was concluded on October 19. Poojya Shri Gurupadalinga Shivayogi honored all the artists with certificate and mementos. Twelve artists from different parts of the country participated in this mega camp. All of the paintings were gifted to Babaladi math for their permanent collection. The artists who participated in the camp are Dr. S.M .Neela, Ambaraya Chinmalli, Dr. Rehaman Patel, Dr. Vishweshwari Tiwari, Nagraj Kumbhar, Siddu Margol, Baswaraj Korkan, Basawaraj Kamaji, Bhimrao B, Kahkashan Naneen, Sasmitha Maharana and Swetha G. all these artists painted the theme in realistic, semi realistic, portraits, landscape etc.

In the same event the Kendra has also felicitated the artists and photographers Mohammed Ayazuddin Patel and Narayan M. Joshi for their achievements in the field.

Art Affairs

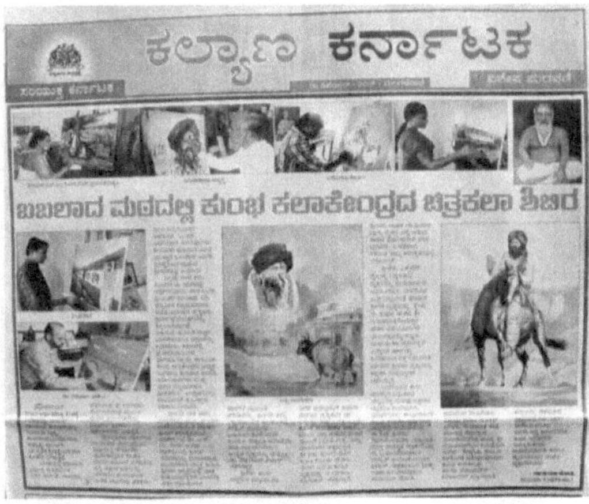

Pottery camp BY KUMBH KALA KENDRA KALABURGI

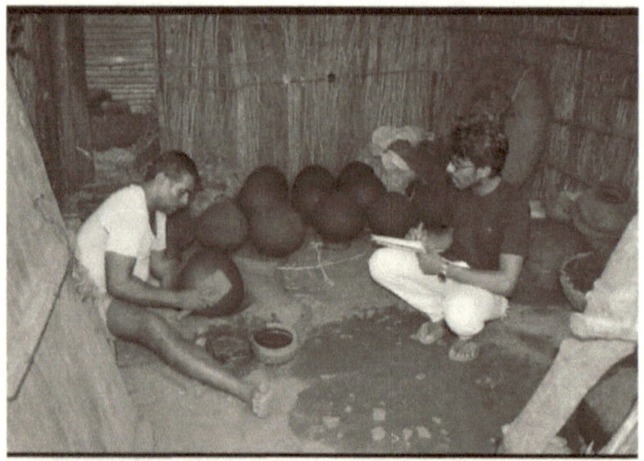

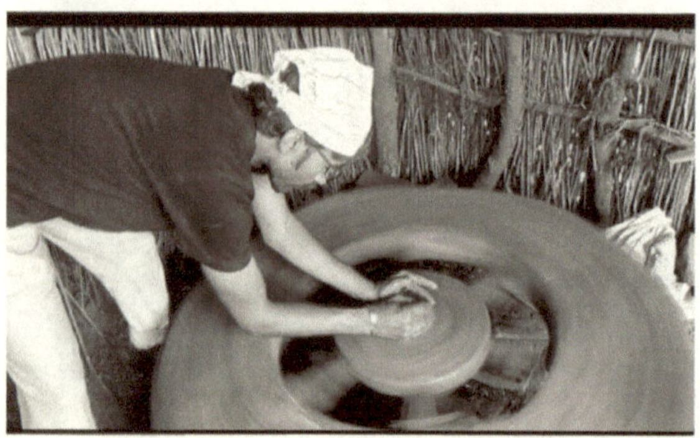

Pottery making camp in aland taluk kavalga
Village organized by kumbh kala Kendra

CHAPTER -5
SOLO EXHIBITION OF PAINTING
ART JOURNEY OF PAINTING IN KERALA: 2011

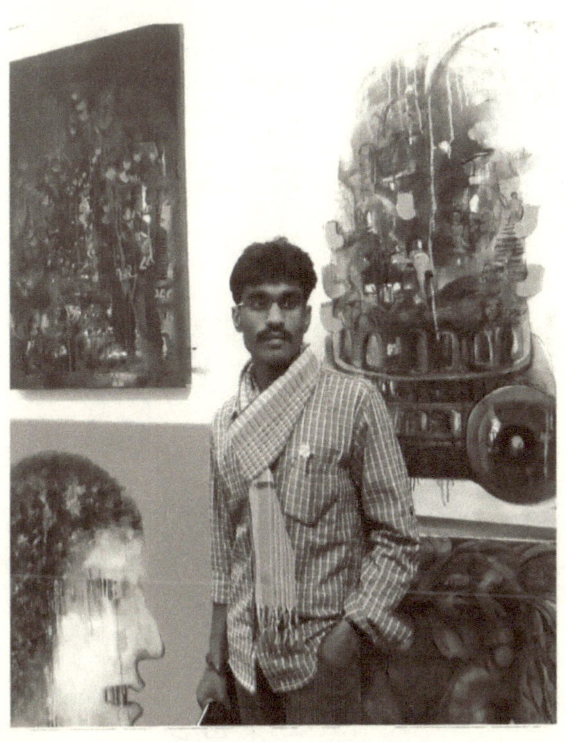

ART VISION...SOLO ART EXHIBITION IN
KERALA -2016

ART VISION

Solo Exibition Of Painting

Artist **NAGRAJ KUMBAR**

ON -05th May 2016 to 10th May 2016

Inauguration
Saleem Shakoor
Secretary west kochi cultural society and
- Seweretry Iqbal Library Mattancheary

Inauguration
05th May 2016 at 5pm

YUSUF ART GALLERY
Mattancheary, Kochi, Kerala.
Mob: 09847478862

Sposdred By:
Department of Kannada & Culture, Bangaluru
Government of Karnataka.

Acrylic on canvas   "kettle-1"   18x18 in

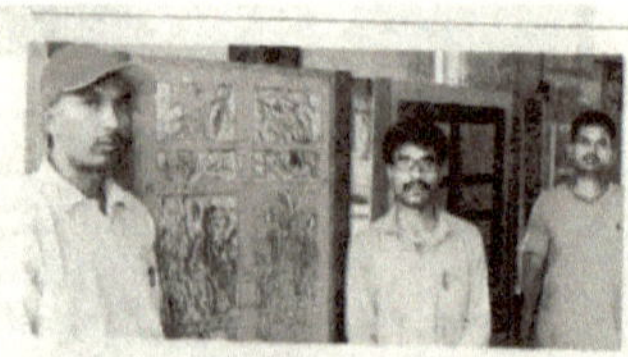

മട്ടാഞ്ചേരി യൂസഫ് ആർട്ട് ഗാലറിയിലെ ചിത്രപ്രദർശനത്തിൽ എച്ച്.
ഹരീഷ്, നാഗരാജ് കുമ്പാർ, ടി.കെ.വിനോദ്കുമാർ സമീപം.

കർണാടകയുടെ
ചിത്രകാരൻമാർ

മട്ടാഞ്ചേരി ● കർണാടകയിൽ നി
ന്നുള്ള മൂന്നു ചിത്രകാരന്മാരുടെ
പ്രദർശനം. മട്ടാഞ്ചേരിയിലെ യൂ
സഫ് ആർട്ട് ഗാലറിയിൽ ആരംഭി
ച്ച. നാഗരാജ് കുമ്പാർ, ടി.കെ.വി
നോദ് കുമാർ, എച്ച്.ഹരീഷ്എന്നി
വരുടെ ചിത്രങ്ങളാണു പ്രദർശന
ത്തിലുള്ളത്.
നിറക്കൂട്ടുകൾ ഒഴിവാക്കി കറുപ്പി
ലും. വെളുപ്പിലും. ചെയ്തിരിക്കു

ന്ന ചിത്രങ്ങളാണു ടി.കെ.വിനോ
ദ് കുമാറിന്റേത്. പത്തു ചിത്രങ്ങ
ളാണ് നാഗരാജ് കുമ്പാറിന്റേതാ
യി പ്രദർശനത്തിലുള്ളത്.
സമകാലീന ചിത്രകലയുടെയും
പരമ്പരാഗത ചിത്രകലയുടെയും
സമന്വയമാണ് എച്ച്.ഹരീഷയു
ടെ ചിത്രങ്ങൾ. കർണാടക സാം
സ്കാരിക വകുപ്പിന്റെ നേതൃത്വ
ത്തിലാണു പ്രദർശനം.

NK an artist biography

GULMOHARA SOLO EXHIBITION OF PAINTING IN BENGALORE -2017

A dynamic artist Nagraj Kumbhar organized his solo show titled gul mohara at Karnataka chitrakala parishat, banglore from May 1-3...some of his creative paintings were on display at ckp financed by the department of Kannada and culture banglore...Some of his noted paintings are kettle, bore, and female related issues were represented on canvas .he is a receipient of human resource department scholarship from new delhi in the year 2010.he has keen intrest in making short films also....

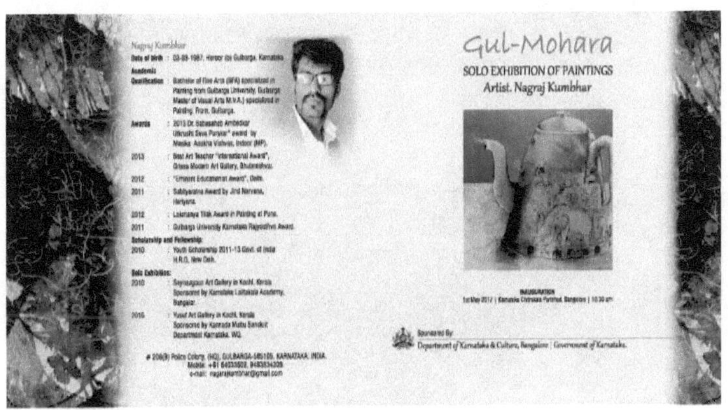

KALAGANGOTRI SOLO EXHIBITION OF PAINTING IN UTTRAKHAND 2018

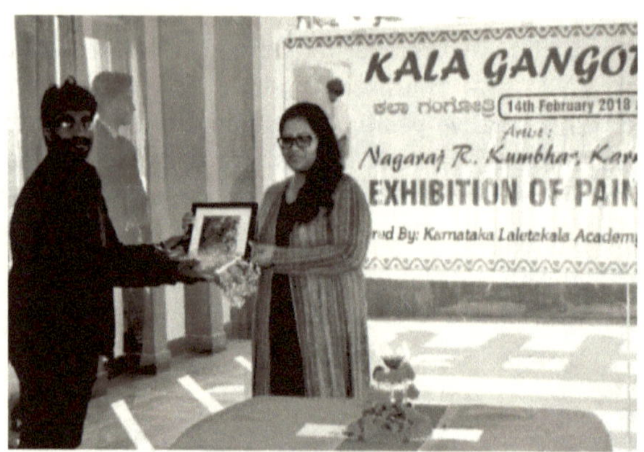

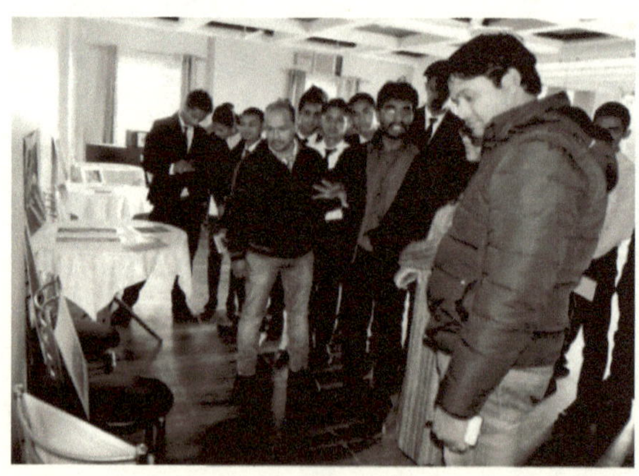

Art exhibition in uttrakhand by artist Nagraj

BANNADA BELAKINDI SOLO ART EXHIBITION IN BENGLORE-2020

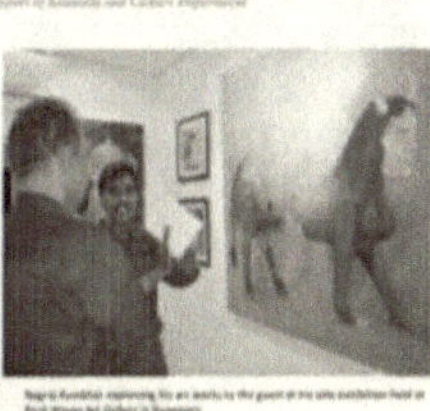

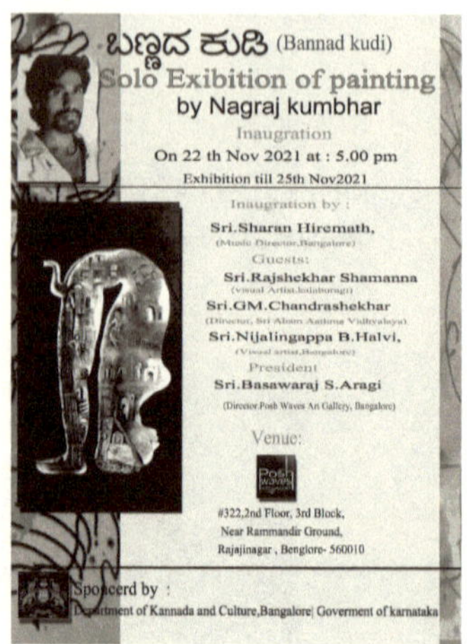

CHAPTER-6

GROUP EXHIBITION NATIONAL
Group exhibition of paintings, kerala

Sun city artist group ,Gulbarga (Karnataka) group exhibition of painting held on oct 20,2015 inaugrated by saleem shakoor (secreatary and president ,west kochi cultural society) at galleria saynauogaon art gallery,kochi,kerala.paintings are exhibit more than 30 paintings of various 10 artist from Karnataka state .vinay palsing (jaipur),sagar   dandoti,vinod   kumar   ,varun jamadar,bheemrao,B.Shweta,padma,narshimha from Karnataka . Nagraj Kumbhar organized this show for art lovers and art buyers promoted to the young artist

Group exhibitions:

2004-2009: annual day of kala mahotsava MMK college of visual arts, Gulbarga 2009: painting group exhibition, chaitanyamayi art gallery Gulbarga 2009: Deccan art society, Founder members art exhibition Gulbarga 2009: painting group exhibition, Ankur art gallery, Gulbarga 2009: mixed bag exhibition, in venkatappa art gallery, banglore 2009:

NK an artist biography

mini art group exhibition, Daira gallery in Hyderabad,2011: all India drawing group exhibitions in banglore,2011: sponsored by panjab lalitkala kala academy group Exhibition in Chandigarh

2011: national group exhibition of painting in kerala Kochi in

2013: Group exhibition in bhuvaneshwar, Orissa sponsored by Karnataka lalitkala academy Banglore, 2012: Group show in Hyderabad inspire art gallery, 2013: Art generation foundation group, Exhibition of painting in kumar swami hall Mumbai

2014: winter Show Group Exhibition of Painting in suchitra art Gallery, Mysore, 2015:"Suncity artist" group exhibition of painting in Kochi kerala. 2016: group exhibition of painting in jaipur, rajasthan, sponsored by Karnataka lalit kala academy banglore..

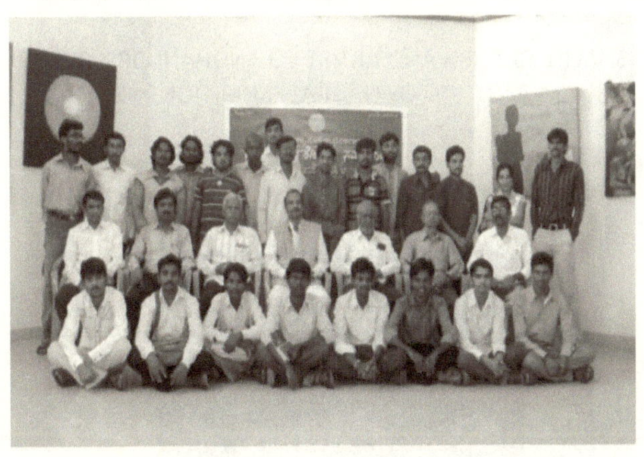

GROUP EXHIBITION OF GULBARGA ARTIST

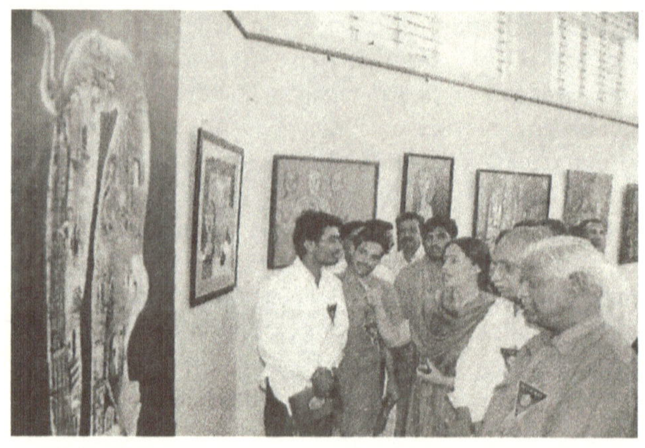

IAS SHALINI RAJNISH AND ARTIST VG ANDHANI OBSERVED
PAINTING OF NAGRAJ EXHIBITION

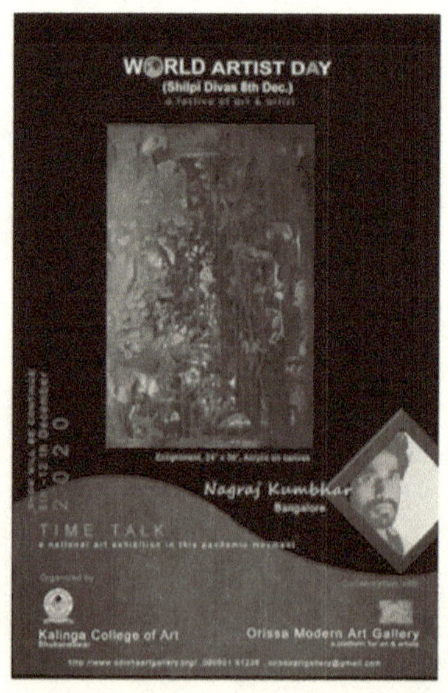

ONLINE GROUP PAINTING EXHIBITION IN ODISSA

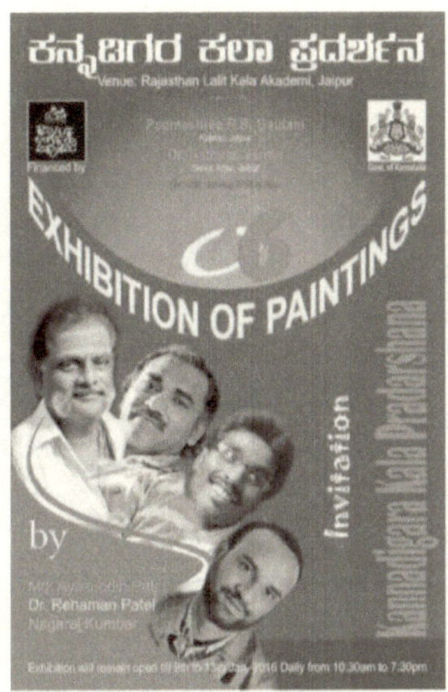

GROUP EXHIBITION PAINTING IN JAIPUR

ARTIST AYAZUDDIN PATEL, REHMAN PATEL, DR.NEELASUBYA
AND ARTIST NAGRAJ

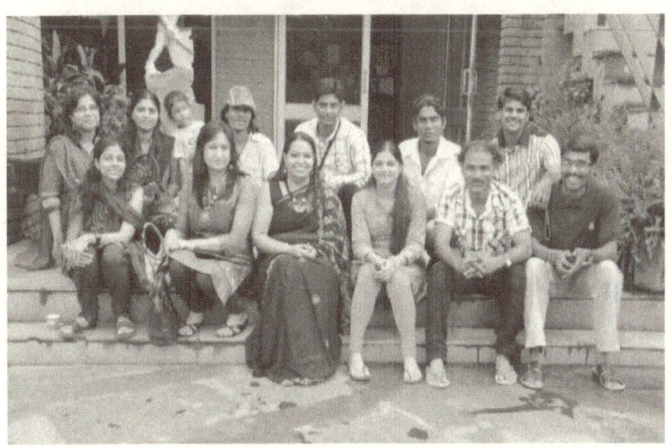

GROUP EXHIBITION OF PAINTING IN CHANDIGHAR WITH NATIONAL ARTIST

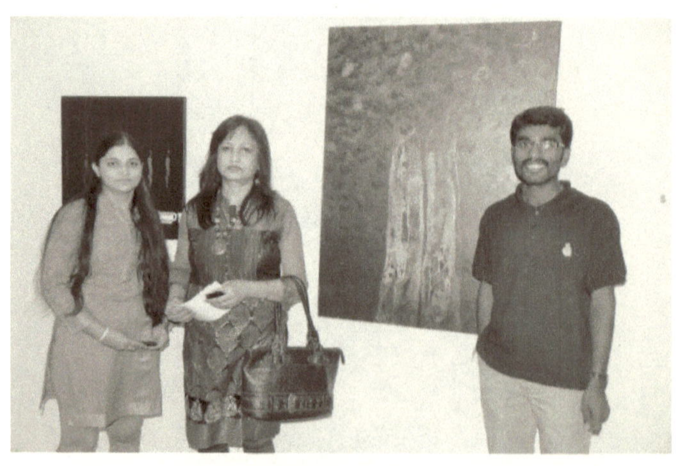

WITH ARTIST POLLY KOUR, SUVRNA PUROHIT IN EXHIBITION IN CHANDIGHAR

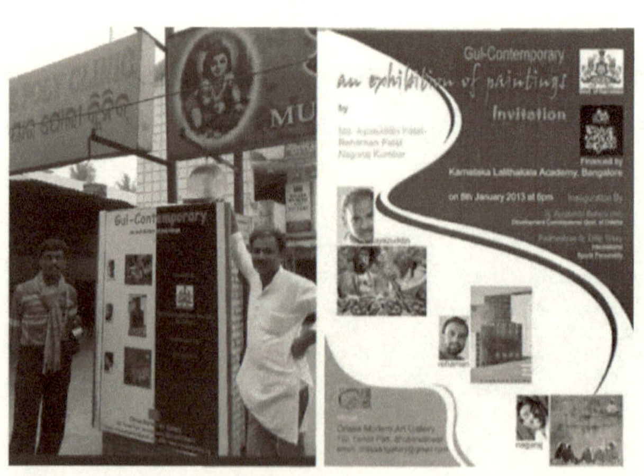

GROUP EXHIBITION PAINTING IN ORISSA
ARTIST AYAZUDDIN PATEL, REHMAN PATEL AND ARTIST NAGRAj

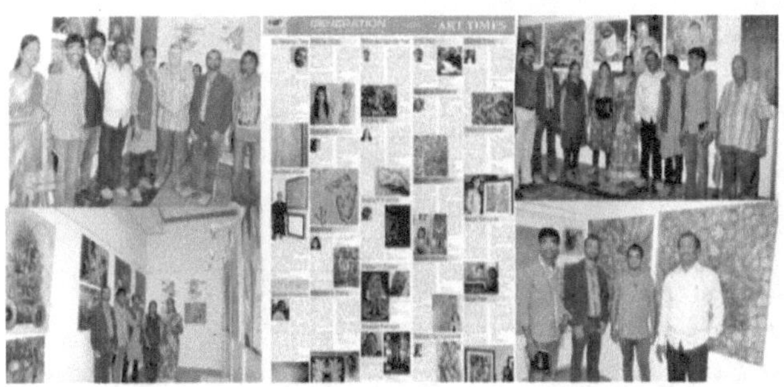

GROUP EXHIBITION OF PAINTING, IN MUMBAI

CHAPTER-7
AWARDS AND FELICITATION

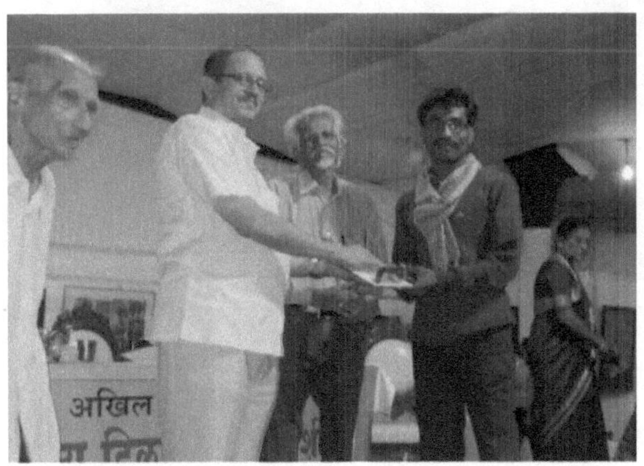

NAITIONAL PAINTING AWARD IN PUNE

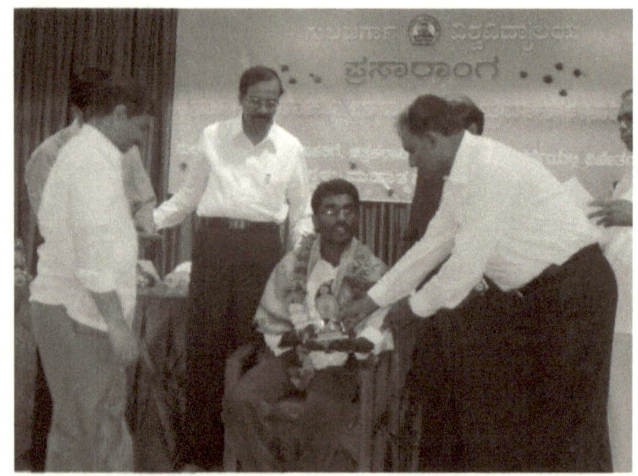

KARNATAKA RAJYOTSAV PAINTING
AWARD BY GULBARGA UNIVERSITY

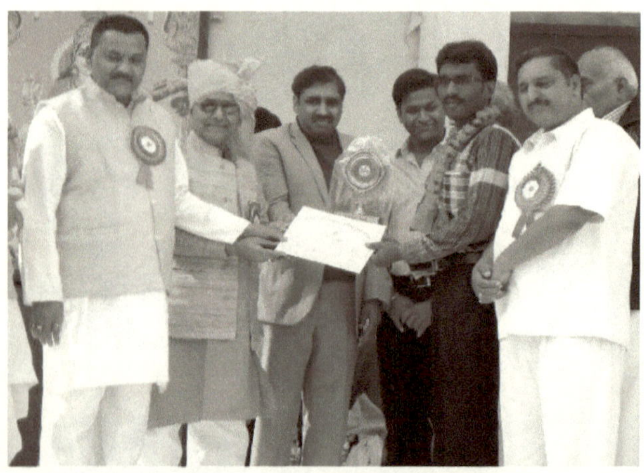

"SAHITYA RATNA" AWARD in JEEND NARAVANA, HARIYANA

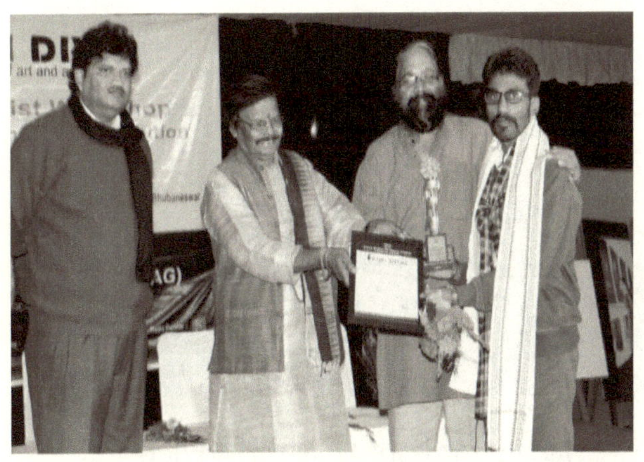

NATIONAL PAINTING AWARD BY
ORISSA MODERN ART GALLERY, BHUVANESHWAR IN ODISSHA

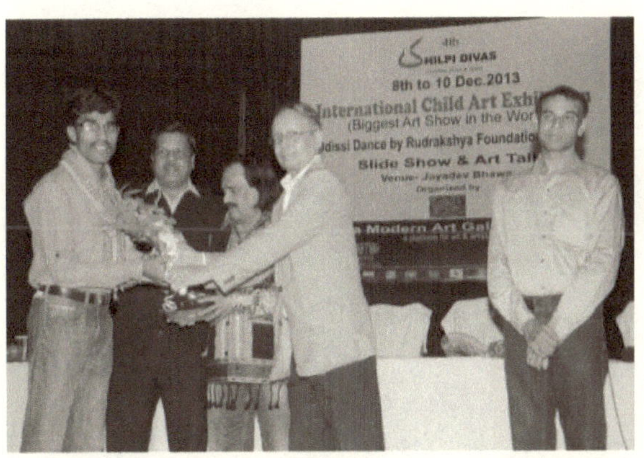

INTERNATIONAL ART TEACHER AWARD BY ORISSA

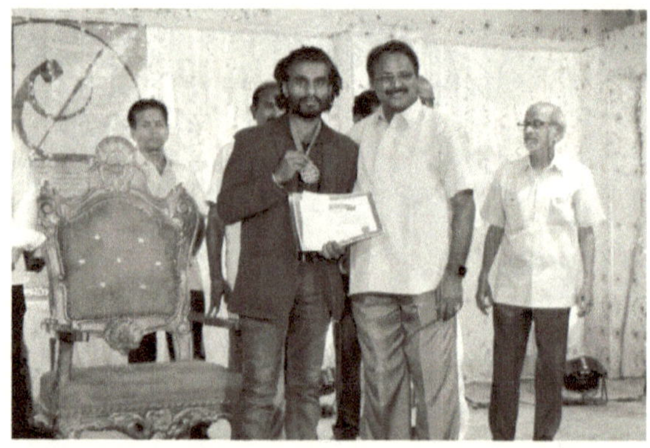

ART LEGEND GOLD AWARD IN PAINTING
BY AMLAPURAM ANDRAPRADESH

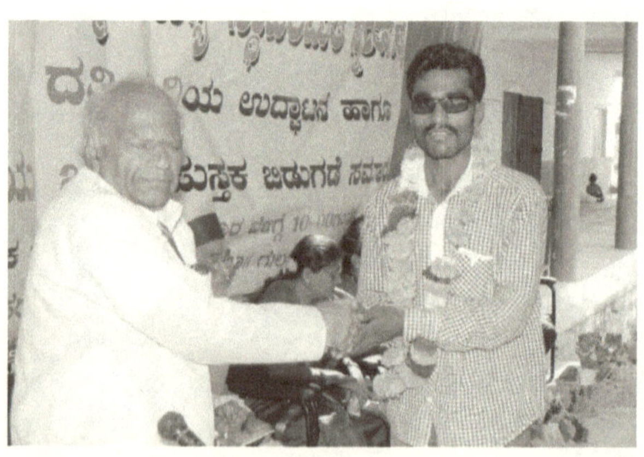

FELICITATION BY GREAT WRITER VASANT KUSTHGI

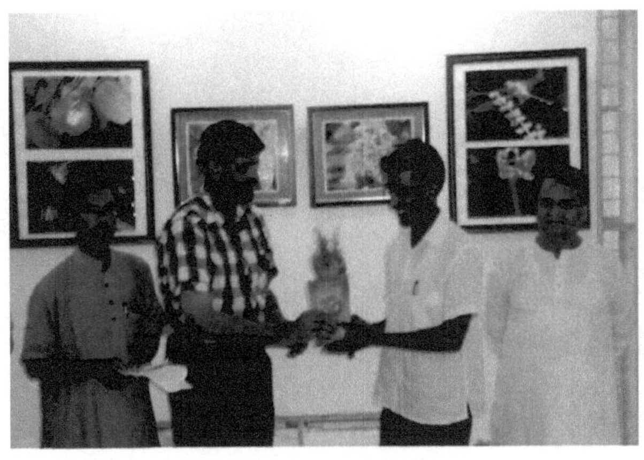

FELICITATION BY KARANATAKA SENIOR ARTIST CHI SU SHETTY

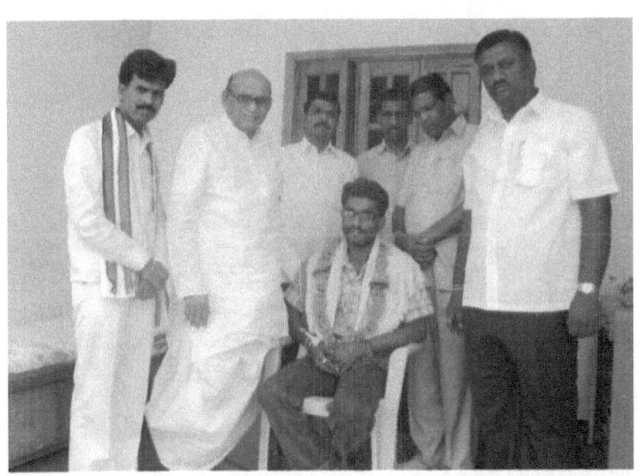

FELICITATION BY KANNADA RAKSHANA VEDIKE AND
VAIJNATH PATIL

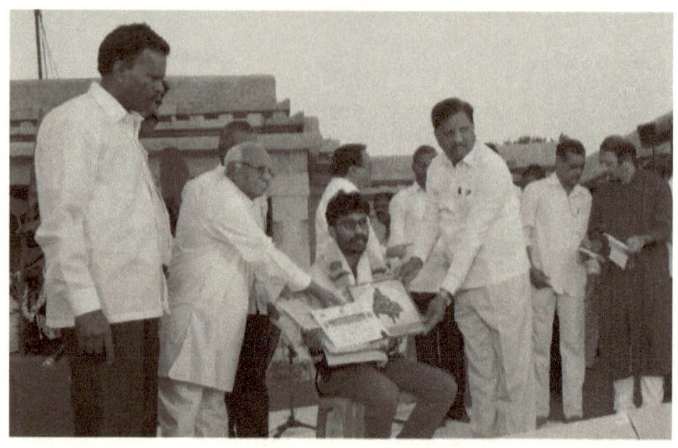

FELICITATION IN PAINTING CAMP IN PULGERI UTSAVA GADAG

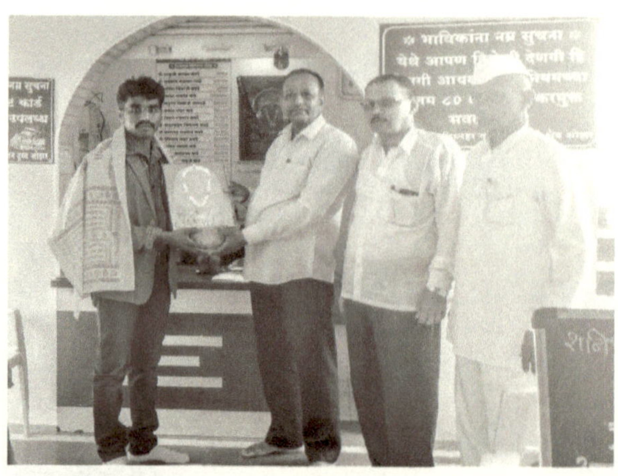

FELICITATION BY SHREE VIGHNHAR DEVASTAN TRUST
OZAR, PUNE

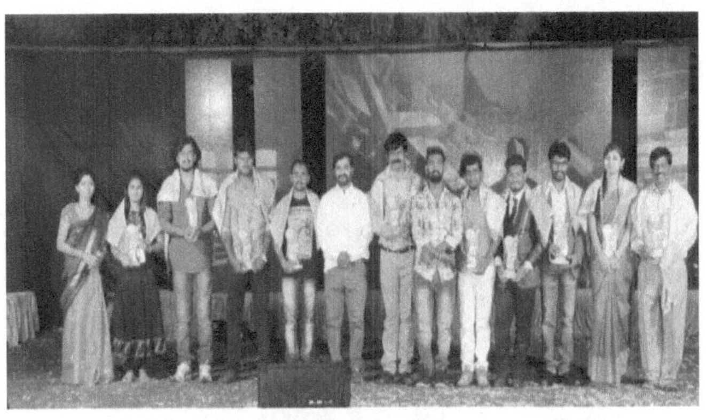

FELICITATION BY YASH INSTITUTE OF ART PERFORMANCE

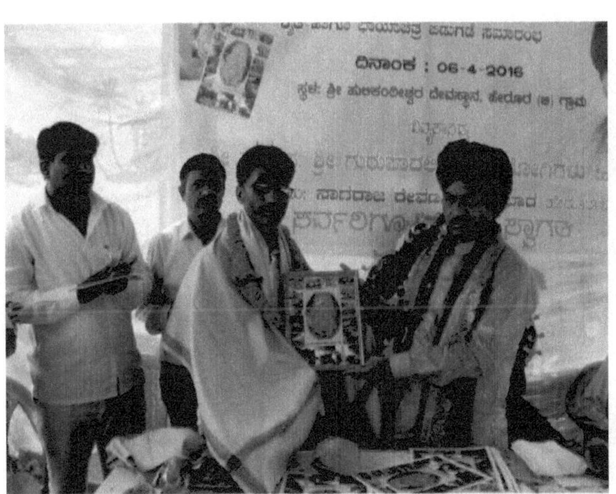

FELICITATION BY SHRI GURUPAD LING SHIVYOGI MUTYA,
BABALAD

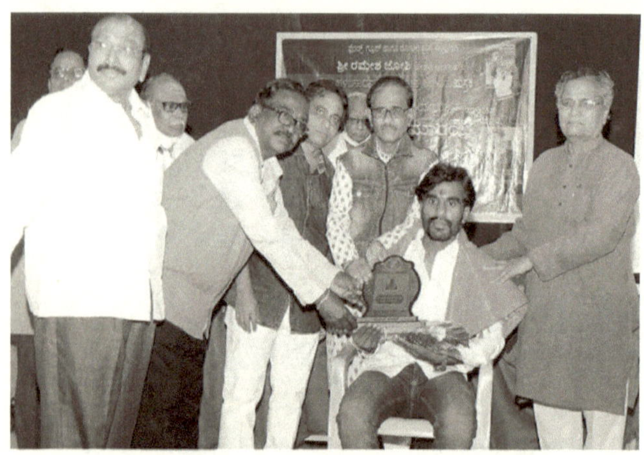

FELICITATION BY ROTARY CLUB GULBARGA
DRAMA ARTIST GROUP GULBARGA

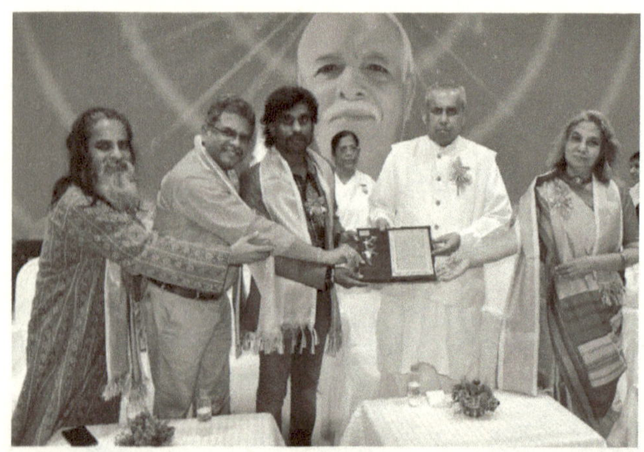

NATIONAL PAINTTING AWARD BY BRAHMAKUMARI MOUNT
ABU NATIONAL   CAMP ON THE OCCASION OF AMRIT MAHOTSAV

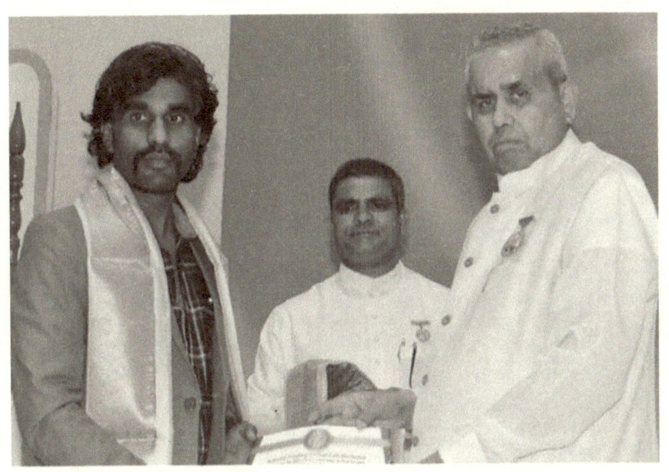

FELICITATION BY BRAHAMAKUMARI MOUNT ABU
NATIONAL CAMP ON THE OCCASION OF AMRIT MAHOTSAV

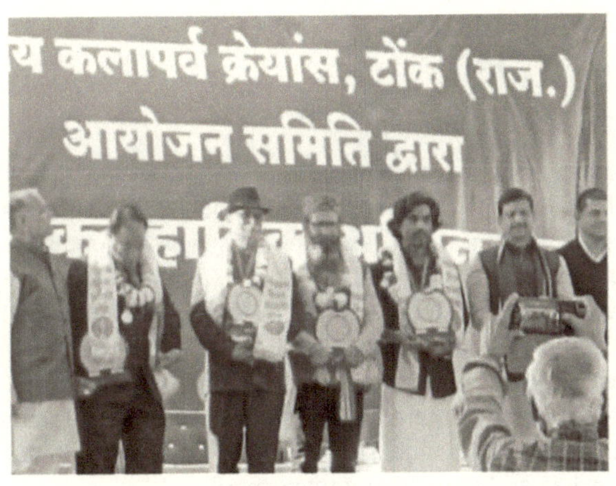

RASHTRIYA KALA RATNA AWARD KALAPARVA TONK RAJASTAN

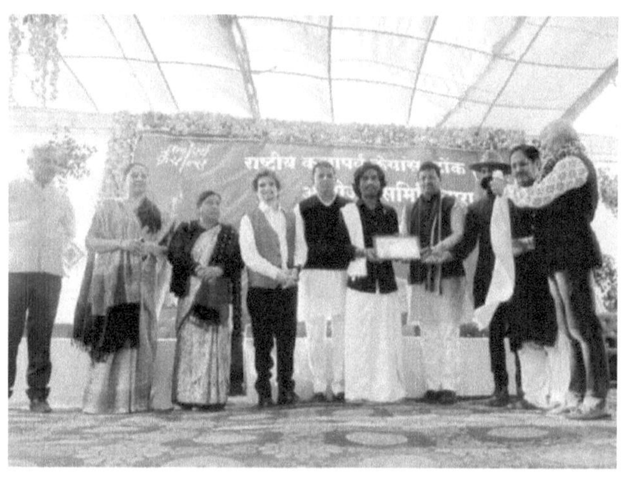

RASHTRIYA KALARATNA AWARD KALAPARVA TONK RAJASTAN

CHAPTER-8
Literature journey

In school days since from childhood he has interested in writing literature from seventh standard .he has hobbies like collection of published paper cuttings, articles, poems, as welll as good thoughts and unique photos.so after then Nagraj Kumbhar impressed by rajendra kumar shedke's good writings in Marathi and he is a Marathi writer.due to impression of this famous writer Nagraj Kumbhar started to write poems in Marathi …

First article of Nagraj Kumbhar published in yuva sakal Marathi news paper and many articles published in other news paper those are lokmaat, sanchar, and tarun bharat many more…

Like he started to wrote book in Marathi, Kannada, hindi..his first book published in "BADUKINA DARIYALLI PRITI"poem published by the legend freedom fighter vidyadhar guruji, that book preface

NK an artist biography

written by great literary vasant kushtagi,from the inspiration of vasant kushtagi Kumbhar sir wrote many kinds of books that is ...In Marathi "TYACHA VATEVARTI PUNAH EKDHA", KALAYANA, SHEVATCHEPAN","KAVYANJALI"..

Some of his Hindi books are "KUCH YAADE"...In English "PAGE 14","ONCE AGAIN ON SAME PATH"...In Kannada he wrote many meaningful books "NAMMURA SHRI HULIKANTESHWAR PAVADAGALU",BABLADIYA PAWADA PURUSHA",
"BANNADA BELAKINDI","KALEMIMANSHE","HALABANADASTU HOLEYUVA KALAVIDA","KALPAVRUKSHA, DAIVA SAKSHATKAR "PAVADAGALU" and "PAGE 14" and more than 100 a Articles published in Marathi, Kannada and in many other language news papers.....

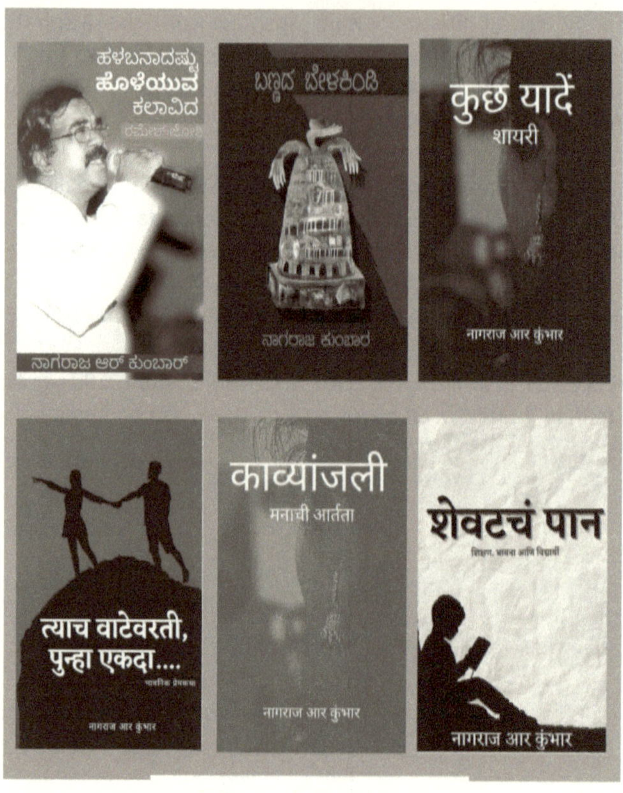

Books written by Nagraj Kumbhar in Hindi, Marathi, and Kannada

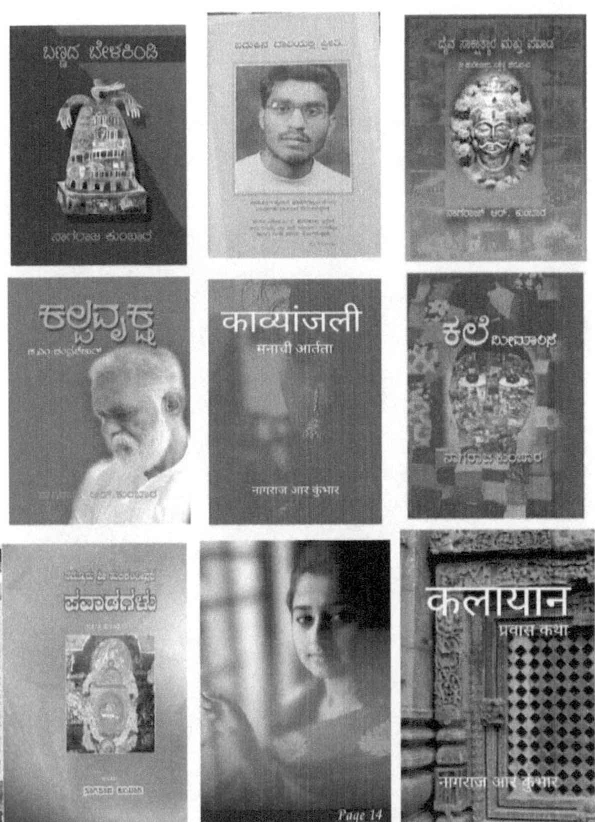

Books written by Nagraj Kumbhar in hindi, Marathi, and Kannada

NAMMURA SHRI HULIKANTHISHWAR..
BOOK REALESING PROGRAMM IN HEROOR B

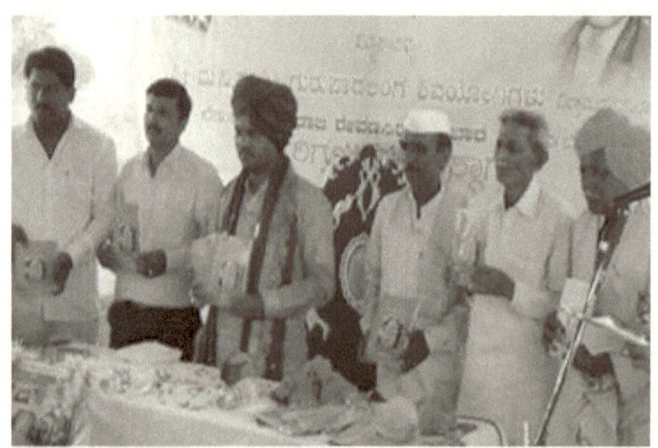

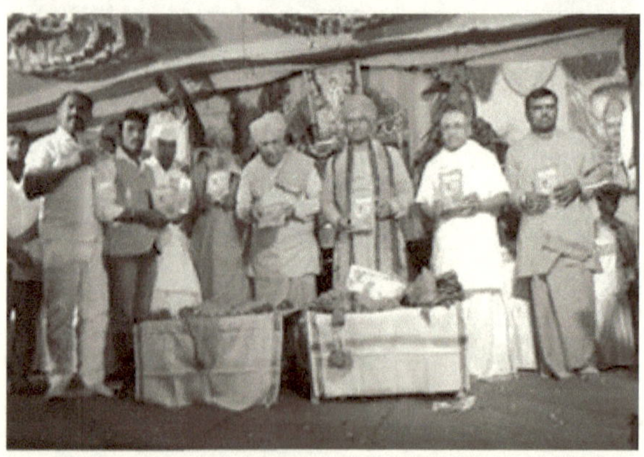

BABLADIYA PAWADA PURUSHA BOOK RELEASING

CHAPTER-9
OPINION COLLECTION OF LEGENDRY PEOPLE
-Vasant   kushtagi Great writer

The blossoming of the talent in the youth ,if it is to be artistically shaped,they should be kept out of secret of love in a healthy way .its value is that if the health is respectful of the taste of the inner revealations in a good and bad way ,it can stand a life of savouring death in all the best statergy .in that conditions ,these love is not limited to three steps,sometimes they go six or eight times and join depths to bring the earth mimes to one place .it is not surprising that's such an influential literature is a medium .in this direction the chutuku genre of Kannada literature is very sensitive ,it is a matter of great pride that it gives wealth in a short time .for the two people who have folklore ,the attitude of poetry and highly influential life churnings in that regard will not remain unknown .in our Kannada bangle ,dvipadi,chaupadis are dharkara garatiras In the songs they are found in the traditional songs of the janapadi .not only are the linguistic semantic riches striking as a result of not being popular,but in this regard vachanas of sarvajna are featured in literature....

Now at the base of all these in the latter part of the 20th century .techonological progress ,scientific expansion ,the triumph of ingenuity ,the instincts- mechanism-inventory of a few moments ,the love loves of the original zari of life are to be savoured .weighed down by the abundance of navarasas,we have to make pieces of the great poems one by one and enjoy each piece every now and then and jump back in to business life .in that direction ,the taste of abhyanga bath of love should be sprinkled and life shoud be harmonized in its bed .in that direction ,love haste to satisfy its impartially at that moment .
Vishwanath's speech is a strong confirmation of the word poetry .in that attitude...I was surprised to see my young poet friend Nagraj was gifted with the desire to freely harmonize everything in the handcuffs of love and stress on the innocence of the cow's mind, in their open mind we see ourselves as free people who have kept the goal of all

spirituality, the intoxication of love, the terror of the mind when it is in need of love, the distruction of the underworld as a roar....

This Nagraja's hanigavanas took such a high peak and took a step towards victory .they have awakened the beauty of love in the hearts of small arrows .because sri Nagraj was young .he has a world travel.in that journey he got contact with different languages and cultures .thus he has tried to force everything into Kannada by panchamrita,which convenient in his academic view .the young nagaraj were very concerned about the unity of the nation ,about the spirituality in the world ,who believed that if a man is to be a man ,only love can complete him ,life without love would be trenous.therefore ,for this young man,love has been seen as omkara,the power of nature to kiss men ,the inert spirits have combined it .he saw it with a very holy feeling .if the visible feet of the kissing power are raised there ,the poetic form of nagaraj will not only become very gentle but also the glory of the gangotri ,the purity of this poet's spirit will be known. In that purity of consciousness,
keep singing in memory of this in my absence "Nagaraja's poetic thought in this direction is reassuring as everyone remembers the intensity of the effect of love whenever such pieces are made .they should have frequent brainstorming exchanges to work on a more vocal writing language .be in a hurry for progress but if writing is slowly reduced to penance – the siddhi nadana of blissful attainment is acutely visible to his tears .i am confident that when the lid on that diagnosis is removed .a drop of nagaraja's poetic gem will shine in the veil of the words poetry ,then the effort of this artist (nagaraja)who has carved a sculpture of an ordinary sensitive soul who took the mirror of poetry and tried to make it into a droplet form will come true

- Writer Vasant kushtagi

THE ART RELIGION OF THE ARTIST OF THE ART

Hyderabad Karnataka has been enriched by the rich culture, splendors of a land and great wise men that has been gifted by god many centuries .he has been active in celebrating the culture heritage of the country.Nagraj kumbar is one of those who are growing up in a

NK an artist biography

personal setting.they have involved themselves in this field as an influencer in visual arts, literature, short films, poetry, music.. he has made a break through in the field of visual arts,a language that has made visual experiences in paiting,cinematography and captured images are the essence of individuals who pursue their dreams and culture ideas with a secure sensibility in their careers.sound,vision,music.social experiences in and out of society have been described visually .they are themselves for new and new experiments and are taking steps towards the success of people as a result of such efforts,future will be bright artist community recognizing and encouraging .

Shri Rajashekhara shamanna
Senior painter, kalburgi

CHAPTER-10
MEMORY WITH GREAT WRITERS COLLECTION

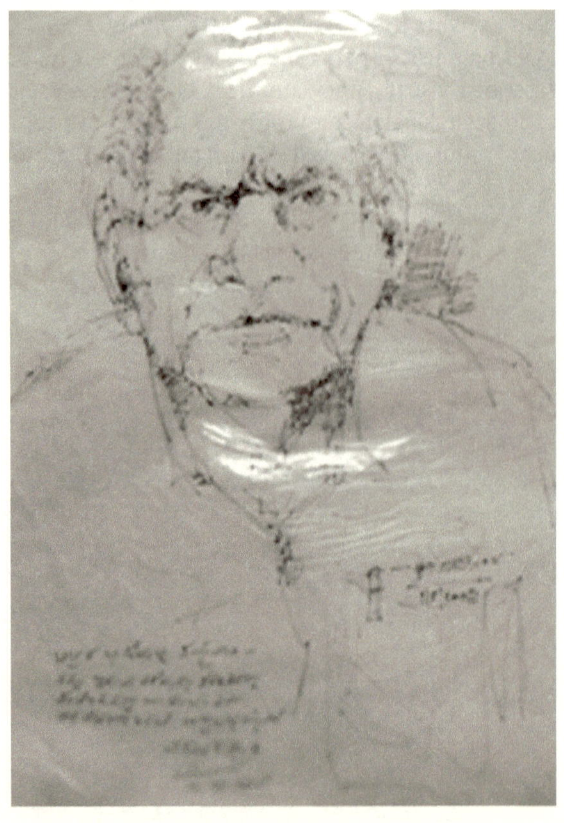

Kannada GREAT WRITER VASANT KUSHTAGI PORTRAIT
BY NAGRAJ WITH AUTOGRAP

NK an artist biography

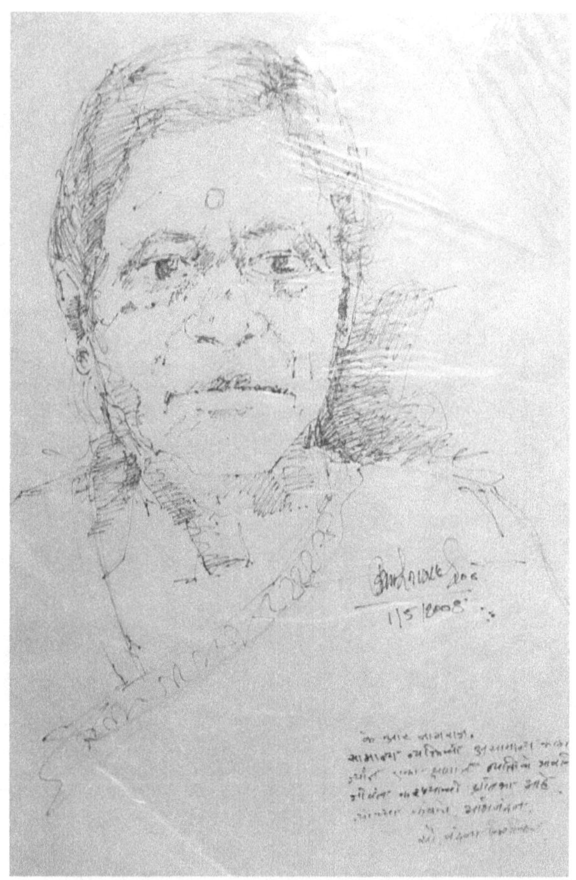

Great Marathi writer vandana kingikar
Portrait by Nagraj Kumbhar

NK an artist biography

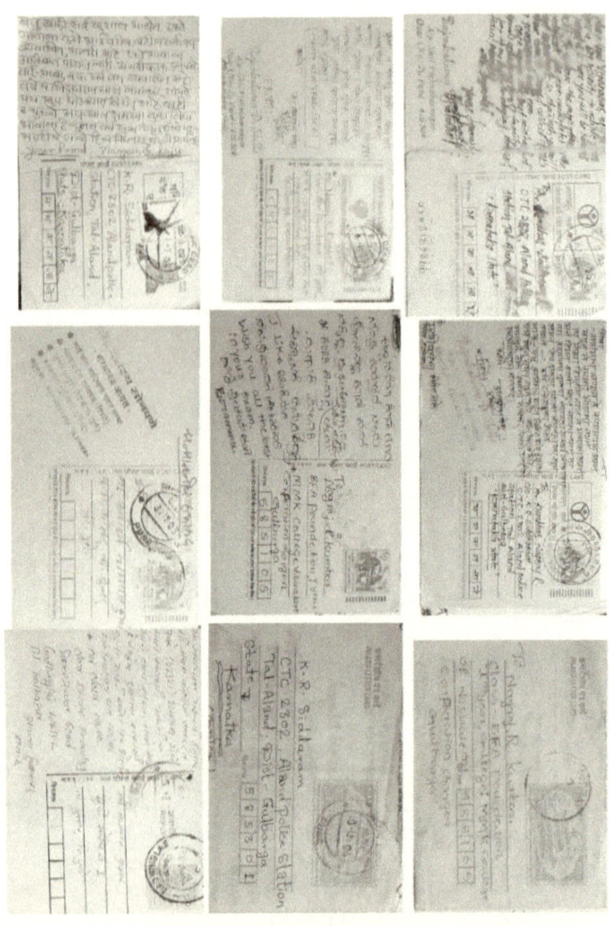

Letter collections of writers and readers

NK an artist biography

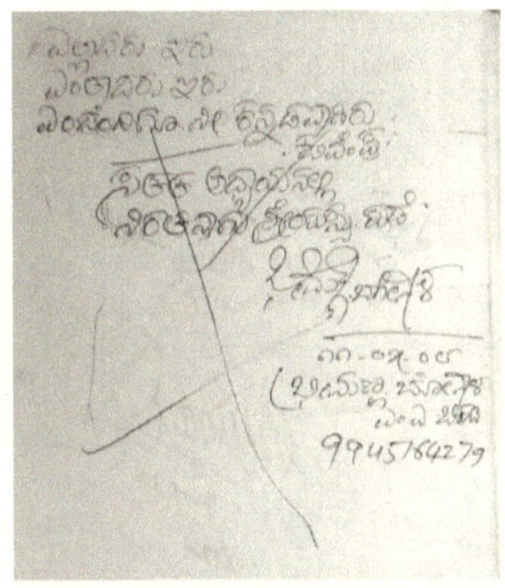

Kannada senior writer bhomanna bonnal

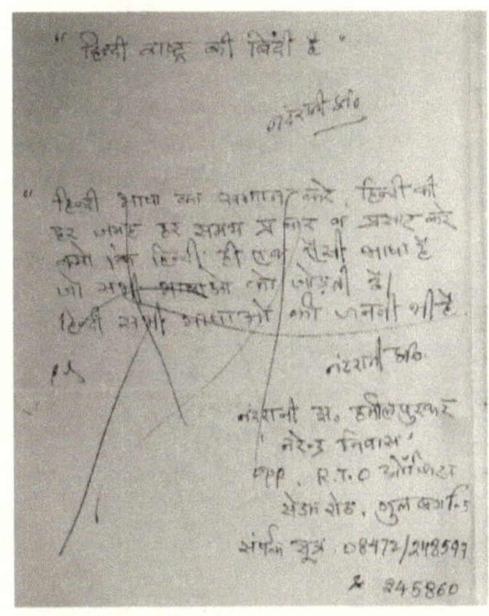

Hindi senior writer nanadrani hamilpurkar

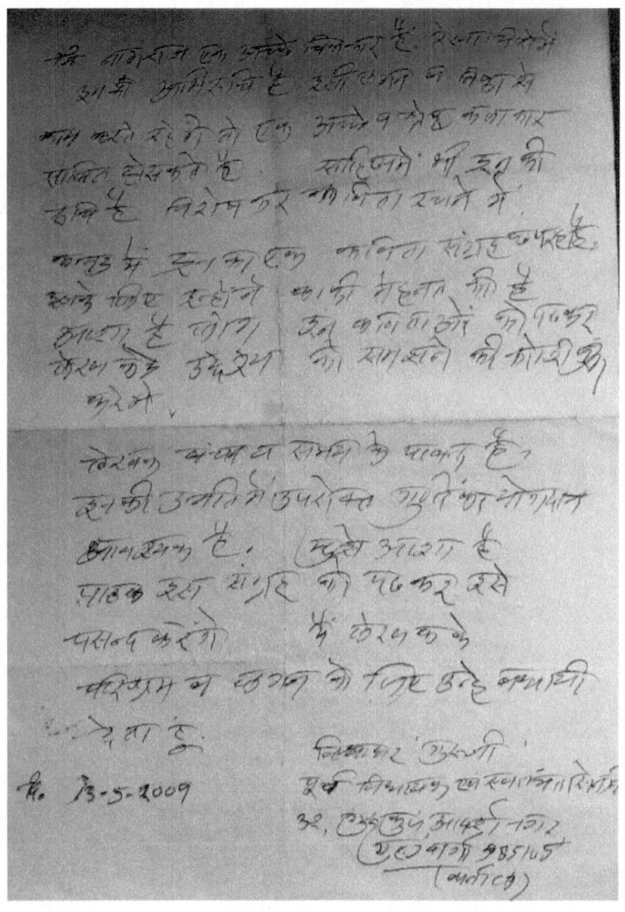

Written by Freedom fighter vidhydhar guruji about Nagraj

CHAPTER-11
JOURNEY OF FILM WORLD

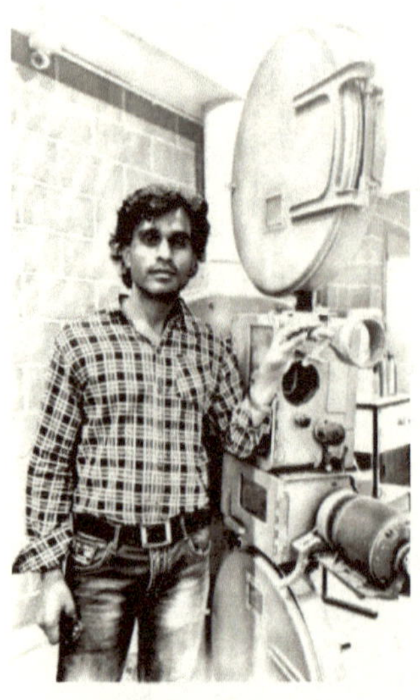

Nagraj Kumbhar since from childhood he has interested in drama, dance, direction, acting...in childhood he used to see and copy others fasion and has madness of using varities of costume collection.he is eager to do things that makes him happy ...due to his poor situation ,he did not come up ..But he has heroism in his blood from childhood.sometimes he used to do drama, entertainment, comic scenes with his friend...he has hobby of collection of hero heroine photos,in those times he has also pics of amitabh bacchan ,madhuri dixit, ajaya devagan..In school days they used to buy the hero photos by the money of his mother when she used to give him while going to school...When he enters fine art college he attended cultural functions by doing script, acting with album song and
Dance...

NK an artist biography

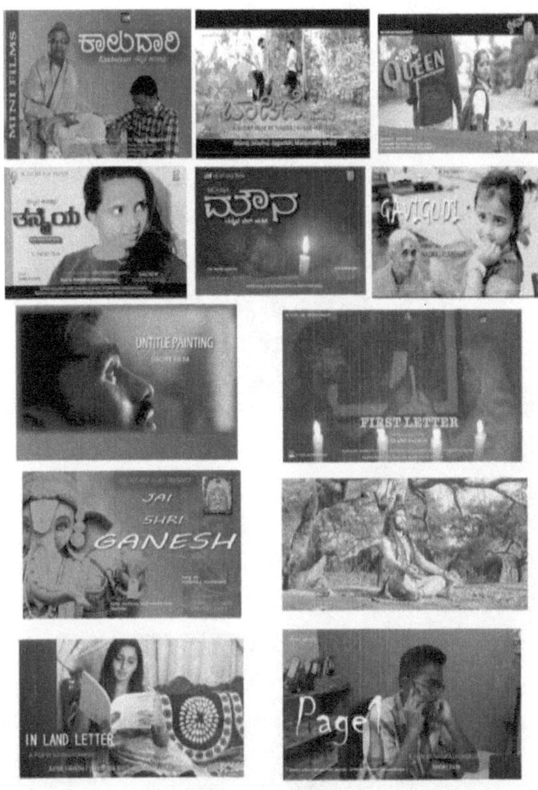

FILM BY DIRECTOR NAGRAJ KUMBHAR

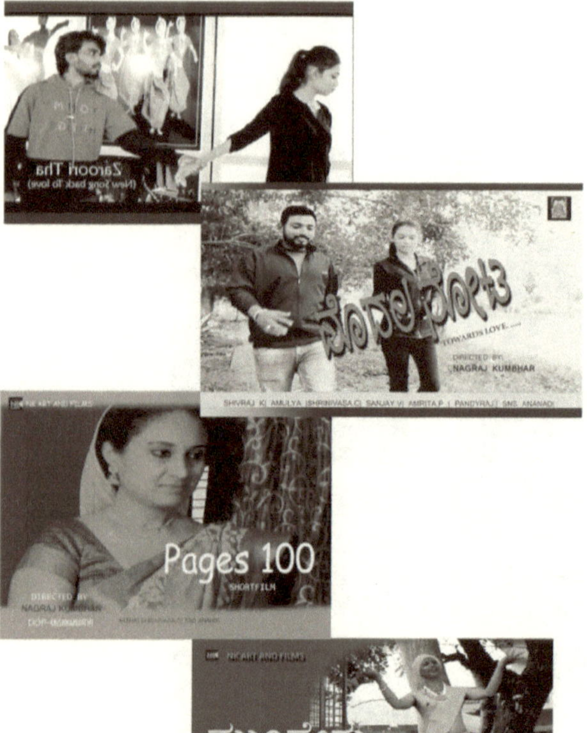

FILM BY DIRECTOR NAGRAJ KUMBHA

he has keen intrest in life line acting...He depressed when he didn't get opportunities and started himself doing short films with his own digital camera...One side art education, on another side he is an international famous artist In between this situation he needs a economic and motivational hands to him...

In scarsity of economy also he didn't give up he done short films...he done documentary on hulikanteshwar heroor(B) village …After some years he completed art education and started journey to banglore fim world …

In banglore one of his friend basavaraj kumbar (udaya tv reporter)sees his documentary and gave an opportunity to release in udaya tv documentary and it comes in udaya tv as in " satya " title he has got popularity in that 'from this he got motivation and confidence ..

2017 from Door Darshan   he got a call and had an interview with kc shivaram and he shared his life journey and some of his experience of life...

His first film as a villain role in ganapati bappa morya and he is art director in this film..with this he acted in so many short film..."queen" (emotional daughter of father), "first letter", ,"untitle painting", "magalalli kanda taytana", ..in these films

He acted as actor...like this as a director he created many short films these are "kaludari","tanmayi","brahme" ,"nirikshe", "blackpen", "mouna" and "gavigudi" ,anland letter and some of album songs are "haadu nannadu dhwani ninnadu" " and "jai shri ganesha" also released … and acted in future films also those are "charge sheet" ,"ninagaagi 2"

NK an artist biography

AUDIO AND VIDEO ALBUMS

Presents by IRAMMA REVANSIDDHA KALABURGI,LYRICS BY NAGRAJ KUMBHAR,SINGER RAMESH JOSHI, AARATI RANJENKAR,RANJISHA KULKARNI,AND MUSIC BY NAADPRIYA AND TEAM.

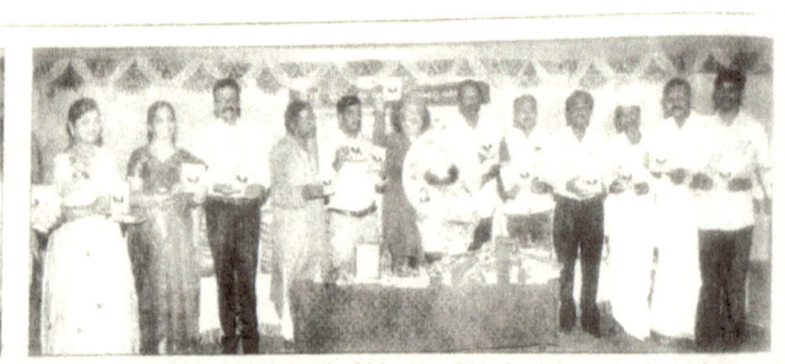

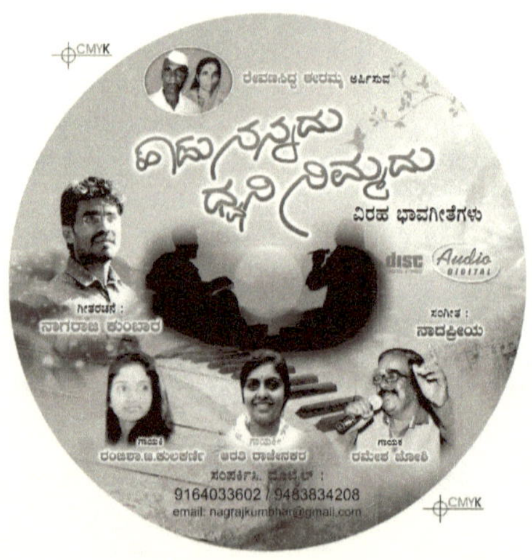

HAADU NANNADU DHVANI NIMMADU AUDIO SONG ALBUM

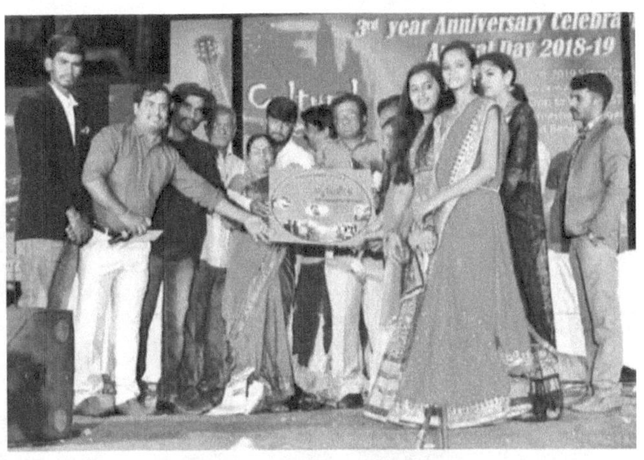

JAI SHRI GANESH AUDIO ALBUM Presents by Nagraj
RELEASING PROGRAME Yash institute of performing arts

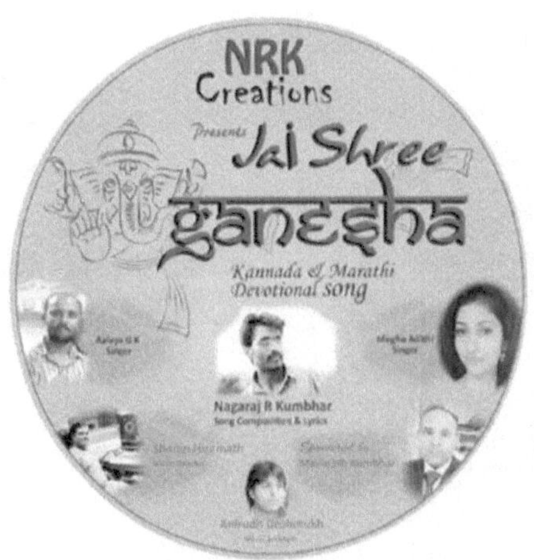

JAI SHRI GANESHA AUDIO ALBUM

Chargesheet movie team...With directorgururaj kulkarni, and dsk prodection

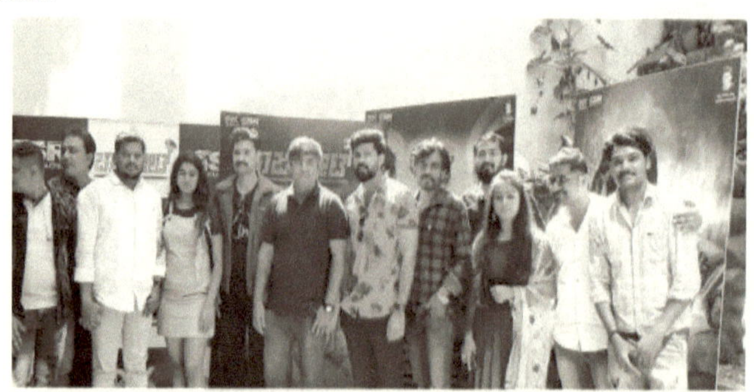

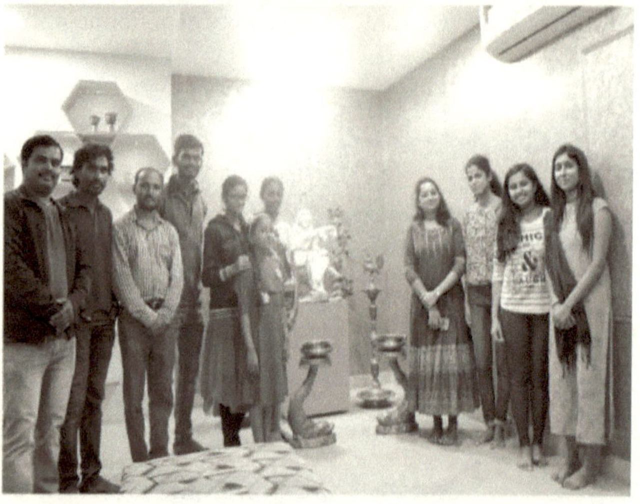

Jai shree ganesha audio album artist team, SONG PRSENTS BY NKART AND FILMS, SINGER MEGHA ADITIGOWDA, GRALAYA, MUSIC AREANGER   BY ANIRUDDH DESHMUKH, SONG RECORDING BY SHARAN H.,

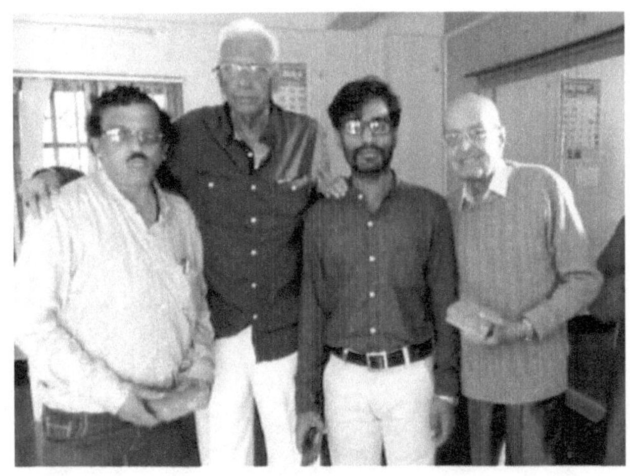

With Director T.Raghu and director Dhore bhgvan sir in special
movment

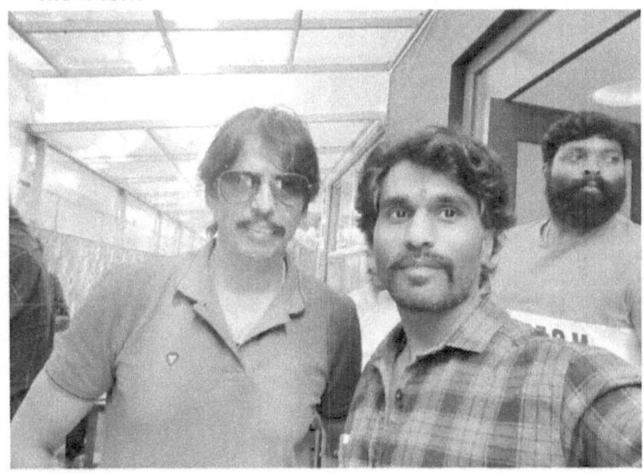

With Kannada actor and stunt master thrillar manju sir
in chargesheet   Movie muhurta cermoney,

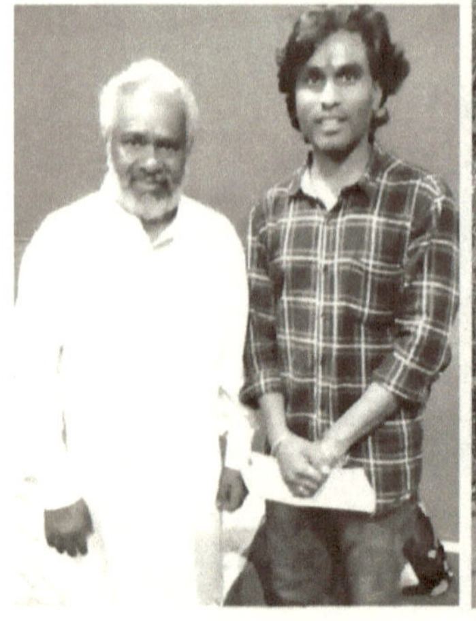

artist gururaj hoskote

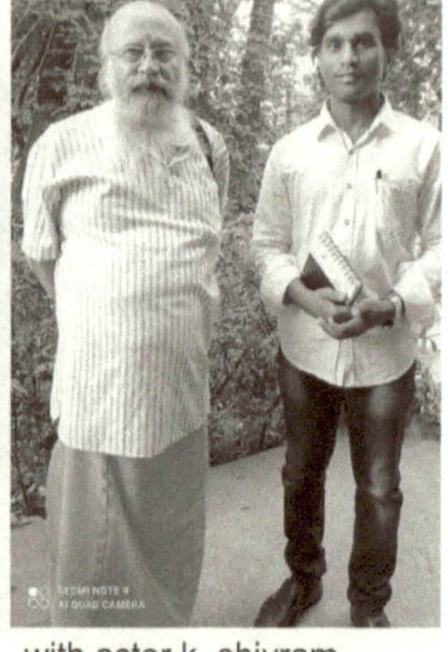

with actor k shivram

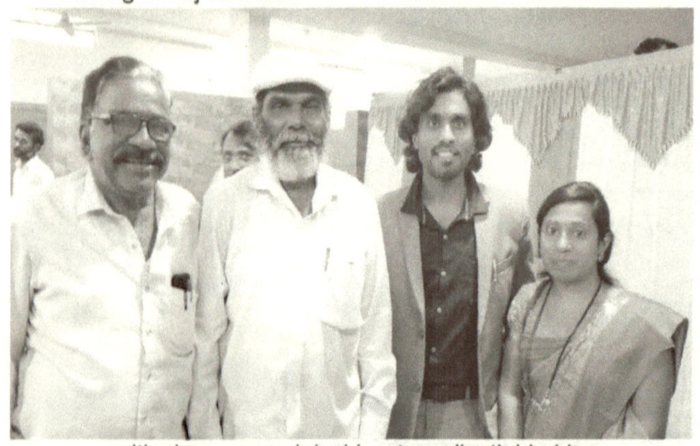

with singer ramesh joshi ,actor vaijnath birajdar

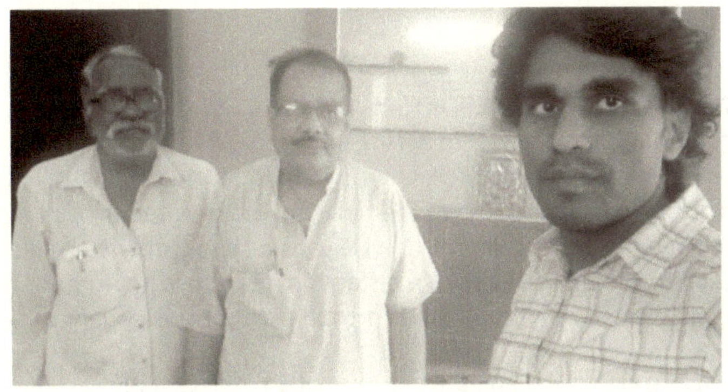

Drama artist and director, and writer hemant kolhapure

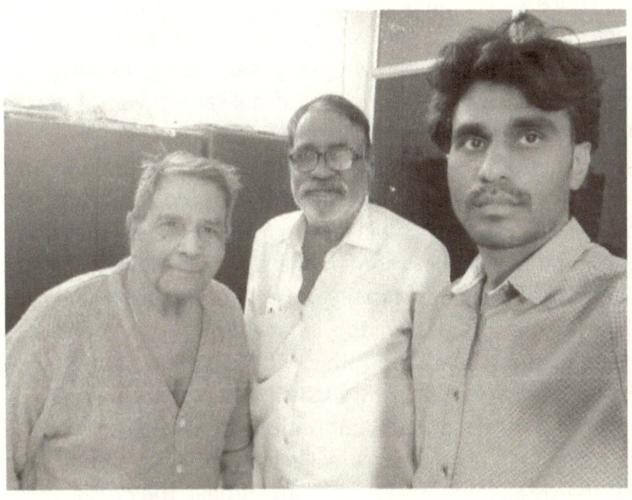

With Malgudi days actor and music director anantrao harsoor

CHAPTER-12

ARTICLES WRITTEN BY REPORTERS AND WRITERS

1. Nagaraj kumbar is a versatile personality:

Artist, poet, writer nagaraj Kumbhar is a multi faceted young talent with a strong rural background, the fields he has devoted himself to kannadiga, he is born in heroor (B) village of kalaburgi district, he got education in Marathi studied in a distant home but has not forgotten writing in Kannada .by that he has proved that there is no language barrier for talent..

A talented artist, although he has achieved a lot as an enthusiast has also taken the adventure of writing letters with love and poetry collection

The love, concern and intrst of Nagraj for the hometown is the god in the village right now, the god who gives form to many things there and inspires the mind.nagaraj who has already attracted attention as an author by introducing the history of hulikanteshwar of heroor is now famous and have succeded Babaladi has effectively propogated the life, miracles and social environment of his..it is the wish of the Nagraj that the knowledge of the story of the gurupadalingeshwara , yogi an environmental lover will lead to many miracles (Shesamurthy avadhani) Rural life will be recorded only if writers develop an intrest in the life of the rural people,their god ,belief,settlement ,and culture through a magnifying glass.in the   many dimensions there expose themselves to the whole world .this work is a being done by artist ,poet ,writer nagaraj Kumbhar through his paitings and articles…

May nagaraj potter's literary cultivation sprout green and grow proudly; many such documents of village life take form his pen! it is a wish that the views there are works of art through the brush..

-Sheshamurthy avadhani

Editor, Kannada prabha, Kannada dinpatrike

2. An illustration of the idea-Surekha hegde

Artist nagaraj kumbar is not pretentious .there is an abundance of colours in the images of his thoughts ,images of nature ,life ,politics ,satire   and future dreams bloom in his brushAn exhibition of

NK an artist biography

kalburgi's Nagraja's paintings"gool mohara"will be held at the Chitrakala parishad till may 3.

A borawelll film created by nagaraja five years ago catches the eye in this exhibition.we are creating many problems in the name of development which cannot be solved this from film kolave shavagal bavi paint is made for today's situation! Nagaraja says.

He drawn a picture of a man's face with a black blindfold .it feels like a picture of hundreds of faces all over the face ,suggesting that there is a stark difference between a man's behavior in the external world and his inner personality

Nagaraja's hope is to make minds think through images.educated in poona,he graduated in fine art from kalburgi university .he has also received dozens of awards for his achievements.

Having exhibited in various parts of the state,he is more interested in painting on canvas ,acrylic,mixed media black and white sketch Since childhood ,he used to draw picture on plant leaves and scrap papers .i used make paints from tree leaves and flower seeds and paint on the pictures in the book ,even during school days the teacher encouraged my artistic ability .it is said that the decision is to take the path of art was solidified..nagaraj kumbar he writes stories in hindi,Marathi and in Kannada and wrote articles for some movies and short films.nagaraja's works of art are in the exhibition where real life size events are more inclined towards art...

He has established kala Kendra of which is the best medium expression of mind .he is doing the work of conversation of different art created by artists ,teaching art to those interested through lessons this organization .nagaraj believes that family and society are the inspirations for his work .

--Surekha hegade

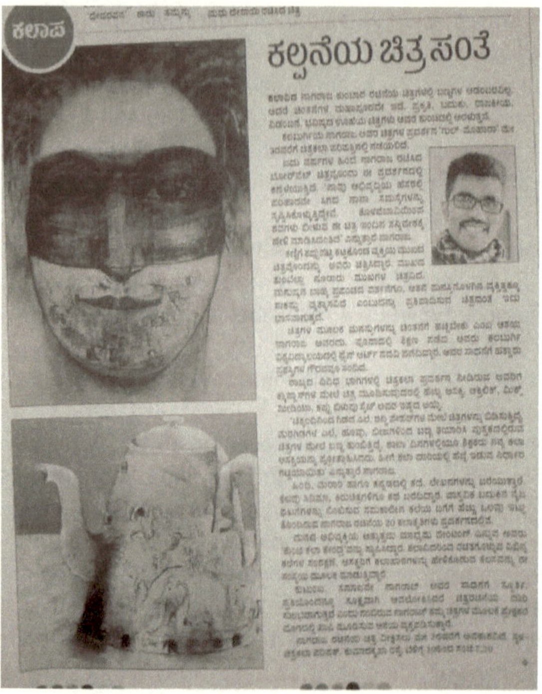

3. A potter who made life in the furnace of hardship. ---
Ravindra s deshmukh

This young man is a proof that there is an aspiration of achievement in a person's life, such a person can all the difficulties and write a little of victory on the magic of success. Nagaraj kumbar at the age of 22 but poverty has already made him a hippie .however he has life in the furnace of hardships, not afraid of this or that he is an extraordinary talent, he has mastered many art forms and he has the urge to strive hard and achieve something

For this ,he is always active and wants there were obstacles to make achievement… Nagraj is engaged in art service as an artist excellent they are enthralled by creating town halls .by creating poetry and stories ,he has impressed the minds of literature lovers .peeps past events that he did not travel and collect pictures of many types of material including rare objects found elsewhere ,photographs ,valuable antiques ,talent recognition ,good books.he has given an opportunity to see what impressive is that he instantly carries out caricatures of typical people he meets .so far he has created caricatchers of hundreds of people on the spot .nagaraja has the distinction of getting shahabbasgir from the lata mangeshkar,india's nightingale…

Famous gazal singer pankaja usman, senior artist vasant phule, senior freedom fighter vidyadara guruji, famous players of literature including hundreds of caricatures of his teachers and friends have beautifully painted with his brush…. Originally nagaraj,a man from Maharashtra ,completed his primary ,secondary and pu education in pune,later due to his intrest in painting ,he came to Gulbarga and joined the city's MMK famous artist and he completed his BA with the help of andani aspires to pursue his graduate studies…

The painter Nagraj,the son of labourer ,had a great intrest in painting from his childhood,but poverty at home made it impossible for him to go to school ,his father went to work …in such a situation the thought of educating children was a dream come true for them .but nagaraj was urge to get an education…

Since then he did not deped on his parents but worked part time in a hotel shop and managed the cost of school and puc college education by himself.seeing his passion for learning ,the shopkeeper also supported him .despite all the hardships ,naagraj had great faith in vishveshwar with the confidence of along with his education ,the support of the society ,where he participated in several painting competitions and won prizes during his graduation from primary ,highschool,further increased his enthusiasm .even then he decided to become good artist .he continued his journey in that direction .the satisfaction of having achieved what he considered a moment of fulfillment in his life by realizing an ambitious dream .participated in many shows ….Indian art culture has a beautiful ancient paintings of heritage…Its greatness in his brush…

The picture created by him have been exhibited in many art exhibitions and some of them have been sold for thousands of rupees .the art of nagaraja kumbar's painting flourished in art exhibitions held in Gulbarga city and mysore, gangavati, koppal, as well as in the neighbouring state of kerala.nagaraj who sys that it is convient for him to express his views..

NK an artist biography

Through painting he has got a unique mental peace.However, viewers feel … This young talent believes that if you experience it ,you will be more happy .he has become a master of literature not only in painting but also in literary creation .kala pratibha has written poems and articles in Kannada ,hindi,Marathi, and most of them have been published in famous news papers ..a collection of poetry titled "badukina dariyali preeti" is published.Shabda shilpi is also serving as the position editor of the Gulbarga section of the curator .to encourage literary activities,chess has established the multilingual kavi manch and organize a conference once a month …. Nagaraj are needed helping hand…he has completed his education through his own work and now he is worried that his dream of pursuing higher education will come to nagaraj the wish and help of the artists is essential in order to reveal his brilliance to the artist.those who wants to donate to Nagaraja Kumbar art service can contact to his number.

- Ravindra Deshmukh

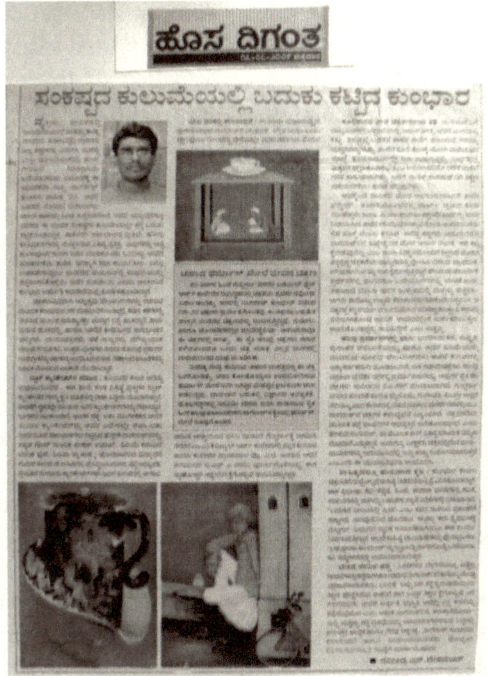

4) BUDDING TALENT ARTIST KUMBHAR

Talent is not in anyone's hand, its everyone's rights ... painting blossomed in the art brush? It is from 1% for talent 90% of continuous hard work, success is yours ....a potter adventure who grown up in poverty and ventures on to the world of painting. He is well known in the field of art.. born on march 3,1987 In the family of a potter in herur(b) village of Kalburgi ,family migrated to pune ,Maharashtra here and there ,the potter who started their primary education in Marathi medium...

Nagaraj Kumbhar ,a potter who came unwittingly ,became a post graduate painting graduate with the inspiration of painting without going into art ,a budding young artist in the Karnataka part of Hyderabad karnataka have emerged .a potter who flourished in painting ....2011 Rajyotsava award of Gulbarga university has recognized the painting talent,later Pratibha kala award ,lokmanya

NK an artist biography

tilak award , bharat vidya shiromani,delhi,eminent education award ,rajiv Gandhi education award etc .he has acquired a vast amount of knowledge   through his active participation in the exhibition of chitrakala   camp art criticism artifacts .knowing five languages ,Marathi,Kannada,hindi,telugu and English ,he has also become famous in the field of literature by writing reviews of painting and poetry in Marathi....

In Kannada too, he has brought out the work"love in the way of life" based on a collection of poems .Nagraja   kumbar ,a budding calligraphy   artist from Gulbarga who has achieved greatness at a young   age   ,has   his   works   in delhi,kerala,Chandigarh,Mumbai,Hyderabad,jaipur,the boy who has exhibited art all over the country without painting images of works of art ,solo paintings flourished in his artistic brush .bollywood film industry's background ,singer lata mangeshkar,madhuri dixit, crazy star ravinchandran ,pradhanta senani ,vidyadhara guruji, solo films by prof vasant kushtagi and international artist VG ANDANI have been beautifully   captured in the story of artist   Nagraj .although the sophistication of the field of painting has declined,it has not lost its existence .young Nagaraj Kumbar says that painters need to be given positive   encouragement ,it is not a matter of words that potters achievements should move forward like a boat..

-BhimaShankar Firozabad

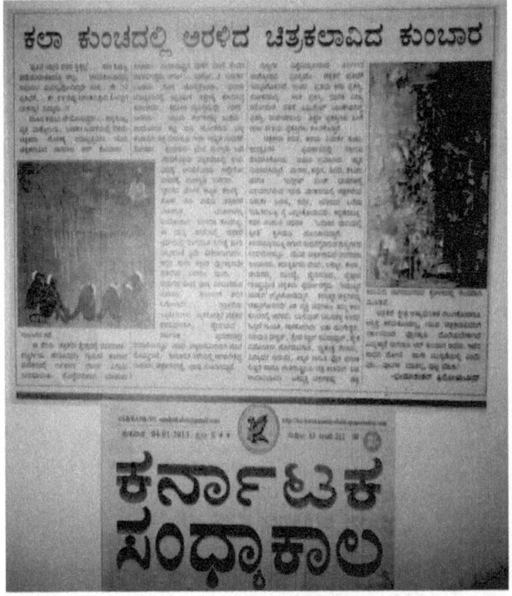

Article written by Kiran patil in Raichur vani Kannada patrike

5) NAGRAJ IS CREATIVE FILM ARTIST

A true rural talent ,nagaraj kumbar of heroor (b) village in gulbarga district in excelling in creative painting with a degree in fine art and a bachelor degree in electrical art ,he aspires to make a special contribution to Indian painting .thus they are going to create something new in film art through creative art While today's youth are mostly involved in internet usage ,nagaraja's love for painting ,desire to achieve something new in it,urge to create something new makes different from others .That is why the pictures painted in his brush have been exhibited in different parts of the state including jaipur,Chandigarh,odisha,kerala,pune, Mumbai, also famous film artists have appreciated nagaraja's painting and painted him on the back Having taken painting as his inspiration .he went one step further and established kumbar art center and worked hard for the development of painting .new artists are encouraged through this center .they are working on exhibiting the best paintings.also,he is involved in social service....

New creation Despite the huge competition of contemporary film artists ,nagaraj has attracted the attention of the audience through his own creativity .what will happen in the future mostly presented in the palm of their hand .social unrest ,rural life and other subjects are his favorite subjects of film art ,till date he has created more than 100 films

Sponsorship of various organizations

Recognizing Nagraja's painting; various organizations have sponsored him and allowed him to showcase his talent .department of Kannada and culture, banglore

Lalita kala academy and kerala state saigaon art gallery Kochi, yusuf art gallery kochi and other institutes have exhibited paintings and participated in painting competitions and exhibitions held across the state .More than 30 paintings have been sold..

 Various awards:

Nagraja has received various national and state level award for his talent.madhya Pradesh indore Dr B R ambedkar utkrishta seva puraskar award,fine painting by Orissa modern art gallery He has own gold medal in painting Gulbarga in college including lokmanya tilak award from pune ,rajyotsava award from university ,he has also received the HRD youth scholarship of delhi... Kot interest in painting grew in childhood.the teachers cheered .So I made this way of life..artists from other states have invited and allowed me to exhibit my paintings .but Nagraj was not satisfied with this. He wanted to exhibit his paintings internationally and he is working hard for it....

-Basappa s kumbar

6) NAGRAJ KUMBHAR IS A CREATIVE PAINTER

Art should be made from raw materials available at home .I want to become an artist for the world with very big dreams. Nagaraja Revansidda, a potter from Gulbarga, who grew up in poverty,is a famous painter ...

He was born in heroor (B) village of Gulbarga district on march 3 ,1987..he was the last son of his father ...father migrated to ast vinayak srikshetra   ojar pune ,Maharashtra where nagaraj ,who

NK an artist biography

didn't know the Marathi language ,was taken nagaraj to primary school ,his guruji bhaskar kaude changed name from nagappa to Nagraj and he went to school   without pen ,pencil or book...he became a potter and made a name for himself .since then he started school in a disciplined manner and studied upto puc in Marathi medium....

Meanwhile, he participated in the painting competition organized by the school and won a prize and got the materials needed for painting .When he needed more,he went to the work of building the grave of the cemetery..

camel award for remembrance film ,prize in competition organized by sakala paper after puc graduation studies Gulbarga mmk college of visual arts ,BFA kumbar of nagaraja art who got admission and got more encouragement .MFA with the   encouragement of anna siddarama,the support of parents and the guidance of art teachers finished later ,he joined Shri Guru Mandir college ,Raichur as a guest lecture and mentored thousands of painting students and went to hampi university as an examination evaluator to gain experience

While learning he did not participate in any competition .he personally participated in various competitions and got it.also participated in art prize camps and actively participated in art review meetings .he also started writing art criticism articles for maneya sakala pathrike and wrote many columns

-Narayan Joshi

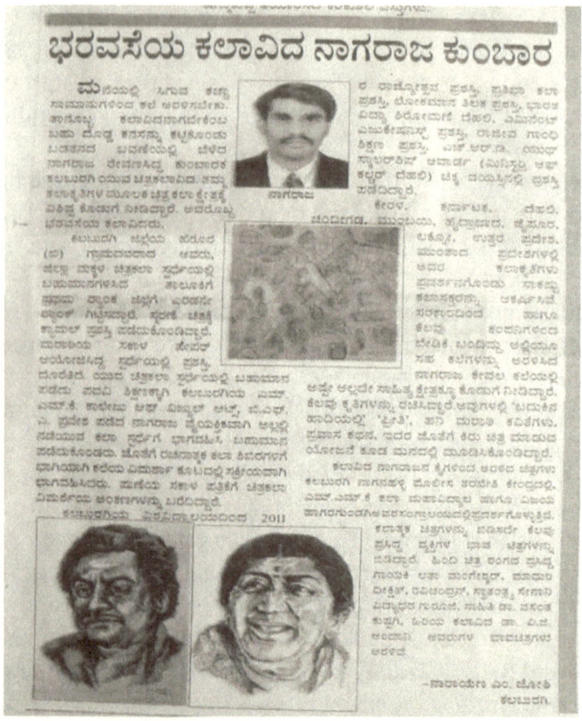

7) Nagraj journey from artistic to filmy world

Nagaraj expressed his gratitude saying that many works of art have been sold His art exhibitions have been shown in places likekerala,Karnataka,delhi,Chandigarh,Mumbai,hyderabad,jaipur,lucknow,uttarpradesh etc have attracted many art lovers .there has been a demand from the government and some companies ,and even there Nagraj made his debut not only in art,but also in field of literature through his works.among them are love in the path of life hindi, Marathi poem,articles,travelogue,besides this ,the project of making

a short films is also in mind....

Artist nagaraj painting are on display at naganhalli police training centre MMK art school and vijaya hagargundgi museum in Gulbarga.they are also sold in germany ,Australia,kerala,banglore,and

NK an artist biography

Gulbarga .he not only painted artistic ,also painted portraits of some famous people .the most important among them are the famous singers of the hindi film industry ,lata maneshkar,madhuri dixit ,ravichandran ,freedom fighter vidyadhar guruji ,the famous literary pro.vasant kushtagi international painter ,v g andhani's sentimental pictures are blossomed by his hands .at a very young age he made his mind to go to different parts of the country with a wheel on his leg .meanwhile,the dream of this painter from Gulbarga ,who has a dream of flying in the sky by plane to a foreign country,may come true and wishing him good wealth

He acted in four short films as an actor .among them he has acted in socially concerned short films like queen, first letter, last painting, page no 14 and gained popularity...a clean short film titled save and raise a girl child ..The message is brilliantly portrayed about the conflict between father and daughter emotions .it has a message that a daughter is not less than a

Son... In the last letter ,it gives the message that love has no caste ,country,language or status illustrated about artists in last cheating .the artist may be blind but art was never blind …it contains the narrative that Similarly in page 14 short film brahma becomes the creator of all of us ,the artist has depicted as the second brahma because the artist imagination is like Brahma ..Presently mr ganapathy is art director and acting in a movie called bappa moriya, anand vatar is the director of this movie, which is an outburst against injustice struggle is a picture of social anxiety...it was short in Mumbai udupi,manglore ,bijaypur and kalaburgi .

The multitalented Nagraj has come out with rich scrolls titled "hadu nannadu dhwani nimmadu"and "jai shri ganesha"..he is a good writer yes he has written many articles in Kannada ,hindi,Marathi language .among them ,an article entitled " love in the way of life ""nammura shri hulikanteshwara pavada charitra and sri channavireshwara charite ,I am a student of babladi bhagvant have been published in Marathi .many artists are the founders of kumbha kala Kendra with the intention that not only Nagraj will grow ,but also others will

Grow by honouring and encouraging artists through activities, they are growing as role models for the young generation

- Revansiddappa hotti

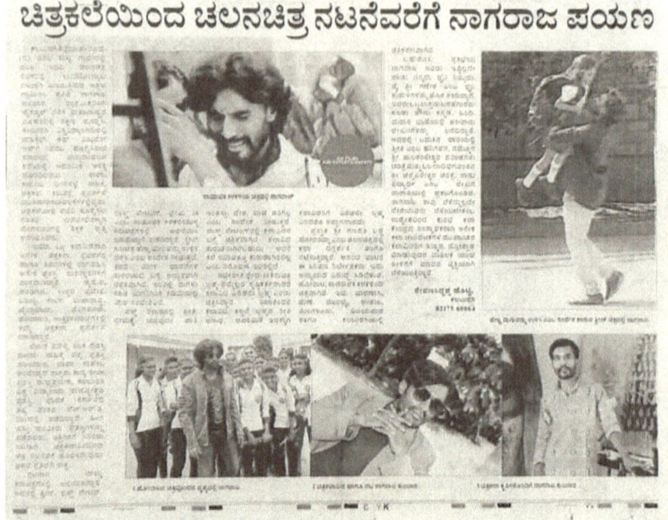

8) Varities of kumbar cups

Making pottary out of clay   is a potter's job ,coming from this professional background he is not a potter .a modern potter who gets creative with colours Originally from Gulbarga district ,Nagraj kumbar BFA ,MFA graduate from ideal fine art college ,is a painter ,has participated in many camps and has been appreciated with the passion of artists in camps   be organized among the young generation…

Depicting all the happenings of society in cups ,these potters have found another outlet foe their creativity .he excelled in portraits ,oil paintings ,modern paintings and terra cotta paintings .cups have painted memorials in personal cups for their cinematography ,the artist thinks that the cup is a symbol of earth or life ,and the images created in it are   strange ..makes the viewer curious .so much importance is given to traditional arts with more emphasis on

NK an artist biography

abstract arts doesnot give traditional arts have acquired their own identity .we are them,They say that if we draw,instead of identifying ourselves we lost in it.

He is a member of the deccan art institute and the development board has shown intrest in buying the work by highlighting it in an exhibition organized by the institute .they say ganakogile lata maneshkar's portrait drawn by him ,lata didi's mind ,drew and gave a letter of appreciation.the fact that this film,which captured lata's passion,now belongs to Dr mangeshkar collection to the artist's youth second prize in gangavathi mahotsava…

Along with painting ,he has a penchant for literature   and has published two collections of poetry.being an artist he has drawn line drawings suitable   for   poetry on every page pictures are more beautiful than poetry.

Lalitkala academy,mani's 22nd 23 rd annual tilak art festival kala gallery banglore,mini art group Hyderabad ,premier talent manglore He participated in major exhibitions .the films of this young artist still have to work hard to attain maturity .due to lack of facilities ,he is working on art .his works need to be recognized by the Karnataka lalit kala academy

-Siddhana gowda patil

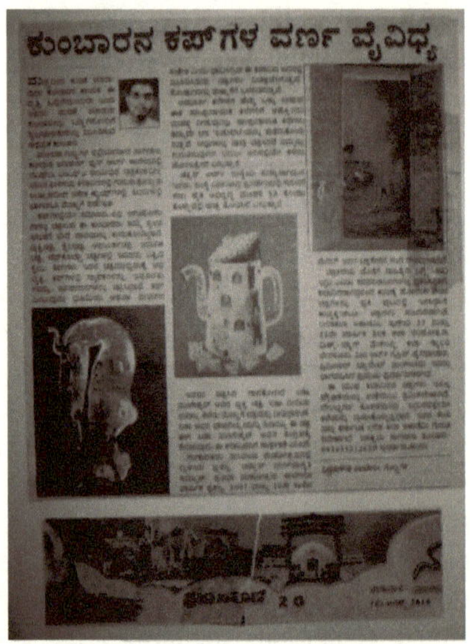

9) NAGRAJ KUMBHAR IS A CREATIVE PAINTER

Nagraj revansidda ,a potter from Gulbarga ,grew up in a poverty with a very big dream of creating art from raw materials found at home and becoming an   artist for the world Born in heroor (b) village of Gulbarga district on march 3, 1987.he was born as the last son of his father and lived in poverty under the protection of his parents.two elder brothers were studying.Nagraj family went to ashta vinayaka to srikshetra ojar of pune ,their Nagraj completed his primary school ,where he did not know the marathi language .his guruji bhaskar gowda ,who was given a   name Nagraj from nagappa…he became a potter and started a school since then studied in Marathi medium till puc

When he was a little boy ,he broke the shell of a battery and took the black colour from the shell and pluck plant leaves,made a colur from that   and paint .all teachers gave shahabashgiri and praise them him because due to intrest in painting from raw materials due to his poor condition   he could   not ask for more materials for painting .sometimes he remembered the words of his father and brothers …at the same time, he participated in the painting competition organized by the school and won a prize and when he needed more

NK an artist biography

,he went to the work of building the player hall and got money from it,took   painting equipment and   paid the entry fee for the competition

Accordingly,the kamal award for the film   was awarded   in the competition organized by sakala paper and in puc was awarded the prize in the youth   film competition   MMK Gulbarga for graduate education after   college of visual arts ,BFA Nagraj got further encouragement for his artistic talent .MFA under the guidance of anna sidrama…he joined sriguru mandir college ,raichur as a guest lectur and mentored   thousands of painter students and went to hampi university as an examination evaluator to gain experience…

For any competition while pursuing degree I was participated in art competition and   got a price .besides participated in creative art camps and actively participated in art critique group .he also started writing art criticism articles for sakala news paper and wrote many columns .2001 rajyotsava award ,pratibha art award ,lokmana tilak award ,bharat vidya shiromani delhi,eminent education award,rajiv Gandhi educational award ,HRD youth scholarship award (mini app cutter delhi) has received   all these awards   at a young age ,he painted more than 100   paintings and won   awards   for   art exhibitions in various districts of the country ….
His art exhibitions   have been   performed in places like kerala, Karnataka, delhi, Chandigarh, Mumbai,Hyderabad ,jaipur,laksdweep, uttar Pradesh etc and have attracted many art lovers ..Nagraj has made a debut not only in stories but also in the field of literature.. through   his works ,where the demand has come from the government and some companies among them are love in the path of life ,"hani" Marathi poems ,student mind articles ,travelogue along with this ,the project of making a short film is also in mind .

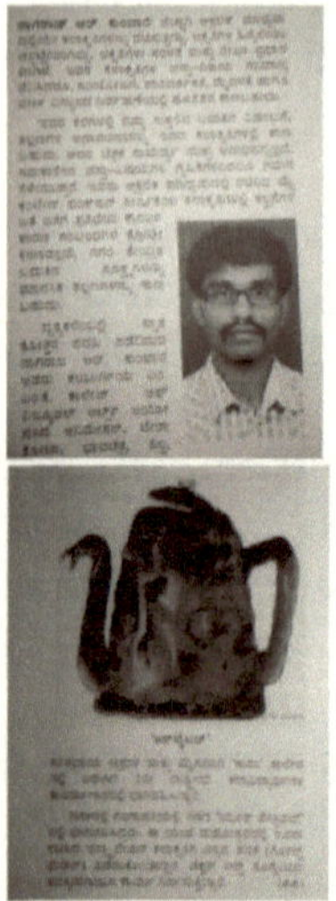

The paintings created by the artists are being displayed at naganhalli police training centre Gulbarga at kala and vijaya sangrahalaya. his films have also sold in germany,Australia,kerala,banglore and Gulbarga ,he has not only painted artistic pictures but also painted portraits of some   famous people ,prominent among them are famous   hindi film singer   Lata Mangeshkar ,madhuri dixit ,ravichandran ,freedom fighter vidyaadhar guruji ,famous literature shree vasant kushtagi international artist ,AG andani's bhava paintings are blossomed by his hands .
at a very young he made up his mind to go to different parts of the country with a wheel on his leg .in the meantime ,I wish this painter from Gulbarga ,who has dream of flying in the skyabroad ,to realize his dream ,to board a plane abroad and bring the richness of art there to the town where he was born and brought u .

PARASHURAM .P

10) Art of kettles, cups and saucers K. SUREKHA
Through the paintings of cups, saucers and kettles at galleria synagogue art gallery Nagraj R Kumbhar explores the saga of life..

NK an artist biography

They are in animate but full of life .the cups,saucers and kettles are objects with which the morning unwinds …imagine life without the piping hot cup of tea with which one begins the day .the emotion and feeling that if stimulates are universal

Tea is part and parcel of Indian culture and its role goes undermined at times through the lifeless objects .human presence finds its way into his works .Nagraj Kumbhar solo exhibition of paintings   at galleria synagogue art gallery speaks about warmth and the better side of life through a series on cups.Nagraj tries to bring out the cosiness that this object radiates .its all about the role of tea in every day life It marks many a celebration sorting out problems making agreements and what not! Nagraj tries to capture the goodness of human interaction over a cup of tea and the hopes and promotes that it offers .the frames certainly triggers dialogue .the objects are symbolic and layered with meaning On one frame you see about seven cups hanging from hooks while on another,cups and saucers are pilled one above the other cups The images trace a personal journey when he recollects his memories in his works and speaks of his journey and destiny Monuments ,heritage sites and the essence of india .its rich culture and sublime spirituality imprinted on his mind during his travel have been immortalized in his works.

Nagraj has not missed out on man woman relationship the sensual and erotic side of life and the storm in tea cup

"I want the warmth of the interaction between man and a cup of tea to spread among human beings .i wants to focus on the positive and beautiful.

Cups in various shaded and shapes adorn his works to show how useful these objects are. He relieves his college canteen days in one of the works In short,Nagraj tries to bring out the meaningful aspects in   the saga of life through these images.reflection on interaction between man and society ,man ,nature and man and his creations are delineated In this works ..Like the images created by Nagraj ,other man made objects and their influence on human beings are explored .the unmindful exploitation of nature has been highlited .on a piece shows the tree of human life bearing two side of life "says Nagraj ,who has an uncanny way of linking inanimate objects and man in meaningful ways Nagraj who belongs to Gulbarga in Karnataka ,did MFA in painting from MME college of visual art at

Gulbarga and is the receipient of many awards and scholarships This 24 year old has participated in exhibitions and camps .Nagraj tries a hand at writing too...He has penned poems with illustrations and written a few pieces on art The exhibition financed by the lalit kala academy banglore will run through Februvary.

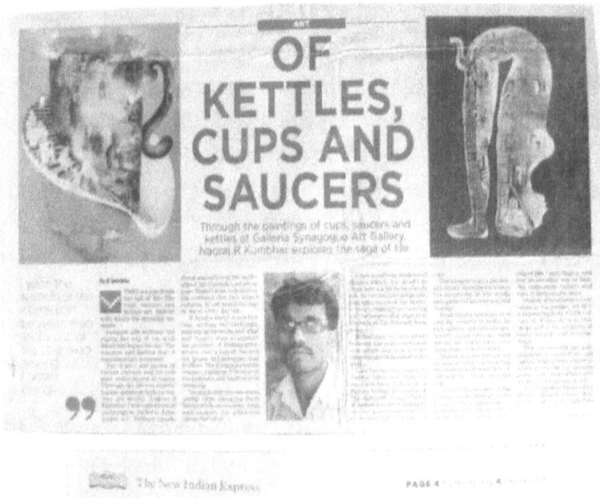

11. ART TALENT BLOSSOMED IN SURYANAGARI

Born on 3rd march 1987 in village Heroor (B) of Gulbarga district in rural environment...   born in a poor potters family.Nagraj got education in Marathi medium up and he lived a normal life with his parents in poona neighbouring Maharashtra to lead a life …coming to academic qualification primary education in jilha shiskhan mandir ozar pune ,high school education shri vignahar vidyalaya ozar pune ,PU college education RA PA sabnis vidyamandir narayangaon ,pune. bacheolar of fine arts (BFA) specialized in painting from Gulbarga university Gulbarga ,master of visual arts (mva) specialized in painting from Gulbarga university Gulbarga.

In ashta vinayaka temple's universal education institute ,he humbly integrated with the help and co operation of the people there and got educated in the Marathi medium ,and used to paint on potters clan craft airani and on yellammana koda even though he lived by doing other work in pottery , painting art came little from birth ,so when he was studying in high school ,he came first in the whole school in competitive painting in art ,from that time he was more enthusiastic and inspired   to continuoue in this way .during this the help and co operation of the marathi people cannot be forgotten .being educated in a neighbouring state has given me the advantage of being able to read ,write and speak Marathi and hindi fluently along with mother tounge Kannada ,also in three languages poetry ,literature and other articles in langauages. Shri B R Dummre and vasant pooje's valuable guidance on one side inspired me in painting…sidrama and shrishail brothers, when they asked Nagraj about his next carrier what to do

 Next? without hesitation young Nagraj from an ordinary family did not have adequate financial   resources for education ,he happily agreed to his education in painting .when he continuoued his education in Y.G ANDANI'S ideal fine art institute with the subject of painting ,he stopped his education due to financial difficulties and later joined with the co operation of brother after joining the post of police ….

Accordingly, the second elder brother shrishail is also educated and working in a company in banglore .education of fine art costs around fifty thousand.. after completing five year course ,now MFA IN the final stage and remembers the co operation and sacrifice of his family behind this achievement … The founder of the institute of art education was the eminent artist mr V G andani's love ,trust ,co operation and power are the reason for the determination.the fertilizer or land of the world is proof of the fact that thousands of students like me are blossoming in this field. Blessed are all those who have received such guru margdarshana from good friend sri anand ,nakhare ,sunil chowdary etc… got inspiration for poetry ,literature,field, and cartoon ,composition etc.

Awards

Second national student workshop 2008,mysore,gangavati youth festival 2008,moodbidri   alva varnajagrati competition 2010 ,2005-2006 till recently MMK animation camp ,terrakotta,potrait ,bittabar   tradition ,graphic, mulak (cement) various   artistic competitions and workshops organized in the institute and got Merit scholarship in 2007 for awards and scholarship First prize and gold medal,silver medal in youth festival at gangavati in 2008 .merit scholarship in 2009-2010 scholarship,2010 kala mahotsava painting award Kava college mysore art gallery 2008 and performance award .since from 2005 to present life conducting various exhibitions every year in an institute... In 2008 lalitha kala academy manglore,lokamanya tilak kala exhibition poona ,mixbag painting exhibition in 2009 banglore,mini kala group exhibition in Hyderabad ,primer talent exhibition in Manglore ,festival art exhibition in bidar . he conducted so many exhibitions around ...due to his talent he selected and he got call for international artist conference at ujjaini madhyapradesh. At Present year 2010-11 Nagraj has been selected for the coaching of sainaguon art gallery...government respects this talent by recognizing them.. painting talent is not come from money,it has to come by birth or it must have come as a gift from god with ...it is a skill of highlight the reality when a scene first catches the eye and it is perceived in the mind In a variety of ways ,then as a line drawing and then painting with a brush ,craftsmanship,perfection of painting is not a learned skill it can only be achieved with dedication and hard work ...it requires concentration ,skill and perfection .thus the artist is emotional in his own right .he is different when compared to other people and he gives enjoyment to people and got satisfaction In that.his art is worth when he is recognized, However, their art become worthwhile when they amuse people and get recognition from them. By conducting few shows and get some money is not much profitable here but also sometimes there is some satisfaction when the response is beyond expectations...Police training centre naganhalli in one of the shows around 10000 demand for the painting is the first step.. .sometimes got disappointment also..When Nagraj draw painting of sriyuta vidyadhar guruji draws 3-4 different styles paintings and prof. vasant kushtagi's film..They motivated and inspired...More than 100 junior students are getting guidance and all of them are behaving well with me, which gives me great support .My education group and fellow students are all friendly and we are all like one family because there is love, help and co operation..Thus,the aid and support of government ,central government ,organizations with their hard work and blessings of all to become a high level artist with the grace and blessings of all of them ...this view shared by Nagraj Kumbhar.

NK an artist biography

- Mailarappa Kumbhar

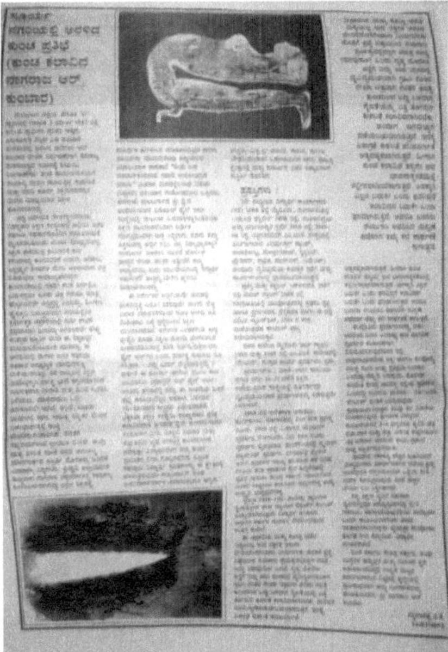

12) ART AND NATURE

all living beings living here are full of beautiful life ,the beautiful panorama of bird flying ,diversity ,art ,earth ,sky ,environment ,seasonal changes and one kind of diversity ..this art has no limits as per the perception of every person .their imagination and reasoning can be found as different ,which has an ancient history even before the human period .there are several methods in this art ,commercial ,natural ,imaginative ,colourful,black and white .all these level depend on the artists sharp eye with many angles .. This topic comes because most of it is common knowledge from lot of news media, reviews, articles etc …. On one day yesterday evening on 29-10-10 at brahmpura kumbar oni, As usual some people sitting infront of a shop .then artist also came and as usual started drawing a picture with a pencil on a sheet of paper…after 5-10 minutes he had finished his work and the young people were gathering around him and talking according to their own opinion .because he drawn pic of that person who he sat infront of shop .someone said told that person"that person shocked to see that there was no difference in his own posture ..and he had never told him when he would paint with such intensity .after that he happily inquired with him , Mr V G sidramappa pujari inquired and got the information about a student of andani fine art college ,wandered around sai mandir ,appana kere and so on … in our city he has shown that he has drawn different difficult and white picture which are real and naturre in different kinds ..giving importance to his suitable mentor Mr Nagraj kumbar ,for the excellence of painting even in today's modern times run a college and given support and inspiration to the talents and let their talent emerge and reach the public …

13. VISUAL ARTIST NAGRAJ -MR. DEVID

God created this universe with his own understanding and really its beautiful to watch and admire the beauty created by God .There are places   filled with colourful nature filled with trees ,plants,flowers ,mountains,streams ,rivers,sea and above all man and mammals both living and nonliving. Beauty of nature is admired by those who are really lovers of nature and here we are proud to write this article about personality who has been admiring the nature of beauty of the things placed on with and adored by the glory and sweet aroma of the nature and captured it into his living life…he is none other than the visual artist Nagraj Kumbar ,who is born on 3 march 1987 a small village in Gulbarga district he was born and brought up in a hindu family and nurtured with utmost care and lore.

He is dedicated in hard working, sincere and very ambitious personality. after completion of his school days in pune Maharashtra from sri vignahar vidyalaya ozar ,after that he became lover of nature he started   living by himself to do a unique and great work to achieve high profile .

He joined   college and completed   his bachelor degree and also secured a master degree in painting .then his dedication hard work he completed free lance artist in professional art field where he was

NK an artist biography

known as sincere ,hard worker and he believed in himself and started his journey in participating in different professional calibration like he   took   part   in   mural   painting   at   various   cities   like jaipur,rajasthan,lucknow,banaras,Allahabad, at various resort on different topics   and different painting exhibitions   at national and international levels and also took part part in different activities .he performed and awarded gold medal and scholarship   from government of india he also took part in seminars at various levels organized by eminent   sponsors   of companies   with great legacy and great personalities like MF HUSAIN and bollywood actress mrs madhuri dixit...

Art talk and slide show of paintings was organized by Odissa modern art gallery ,Bhubaneswar in odisha.where he was awarded the best art worker in   contemporary   in 2010 a solo exhibition was held in kochi (kerala) sponsored by Karnataka lalit kala academy banglore .in which the first painting was sold made by a student   and was purchased by a german art lover.

Some beautiful, colorful, meaningful articles were published in all three language daily news - paper –magazines and booklets. a book was released in poems ,literature,art book about M F husain and madhuris paintings as well as creative art and which contained high profile   and lovable ,readable,sensible ,lyrics which   were admired by all

-Mr David

CHAPTER -13
Letter from the legend artist

Lata Mangeshkar

Legendry play back singer

Dear

Shri R. K. Nagraj

Thank you for remembering me fondly and conveying your warm wishes on my birthday …

The love and appreciation I enjoy from friends such as yourself is the source of my inner strength and inspiration

With these sentiments, I take the opportunity to wish you and your family the best for this festive season

Warm regards,

Lata Mangeshkar

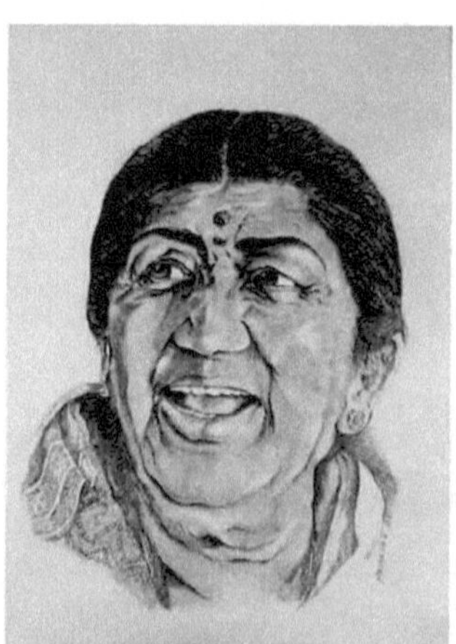

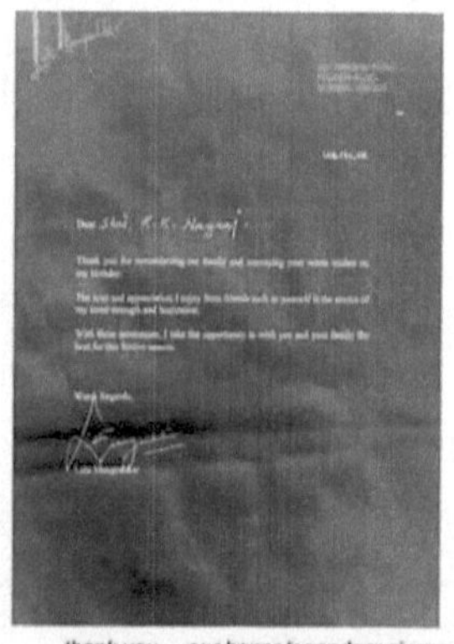

thank you ….our honor legendary singer lata mangeshkar (latadidi) for eccepeted my small birthday gift …

NK an artist biography

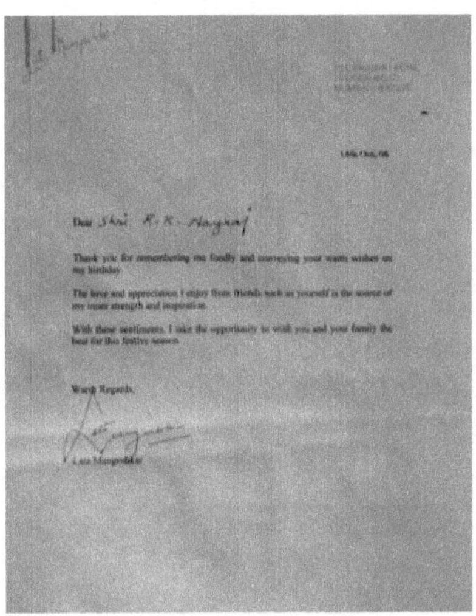

2.   legend playback singer, LATA MANGESHKAR LETTER

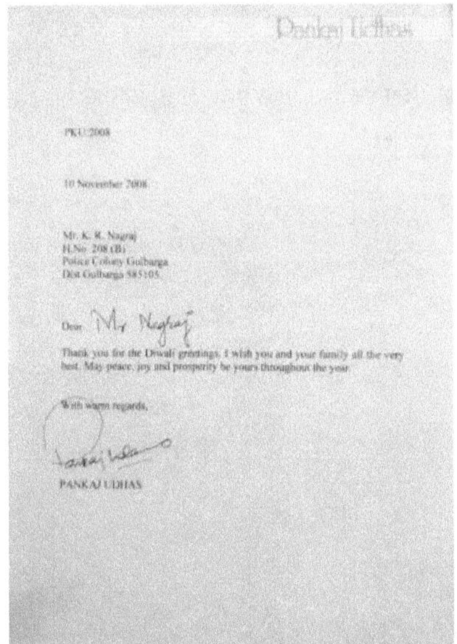

Great singer, PANKAJ UDAS

CHAPTER-14

AUTOGRAPH COLLECTIONS OF an ARTIST AND GREAT PERSONS

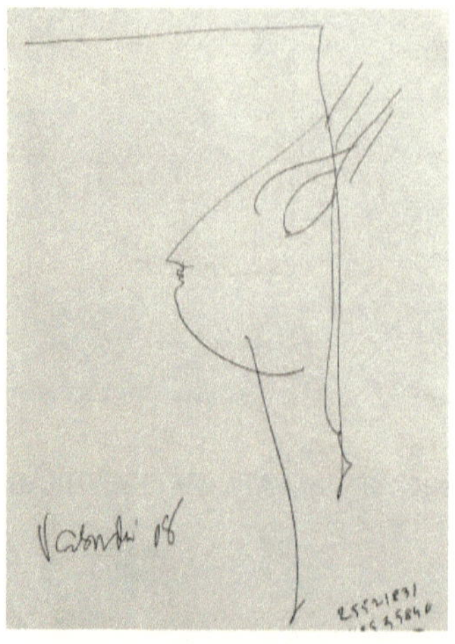

G.s. vasudev Karnataka painting artist

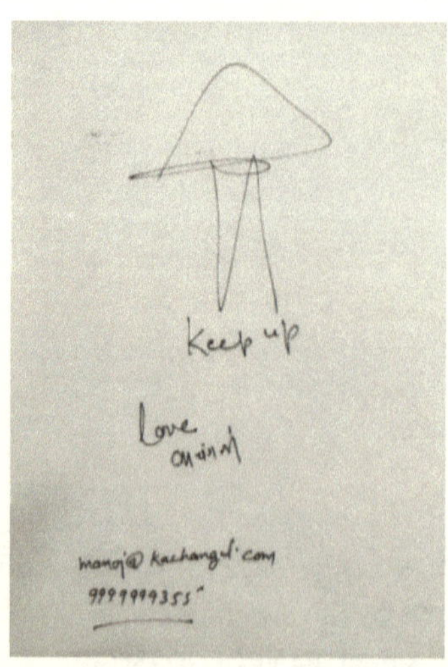

ARTIST MANOJ KACHANGAL

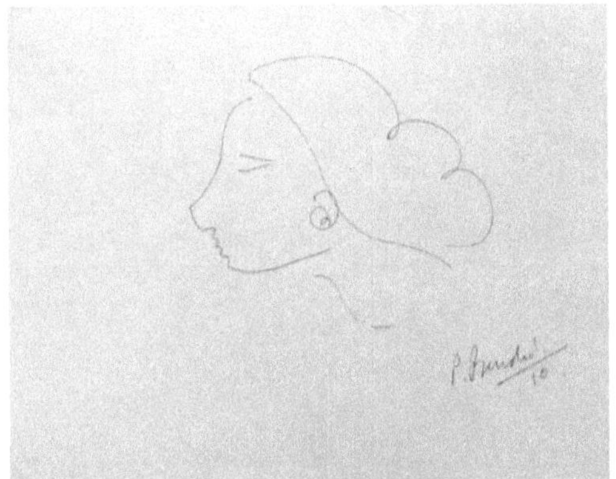

PADBANAB BENDRE AN ARTIST OF INDIAN

ARTIST SHAMSHED HUSSAIN.

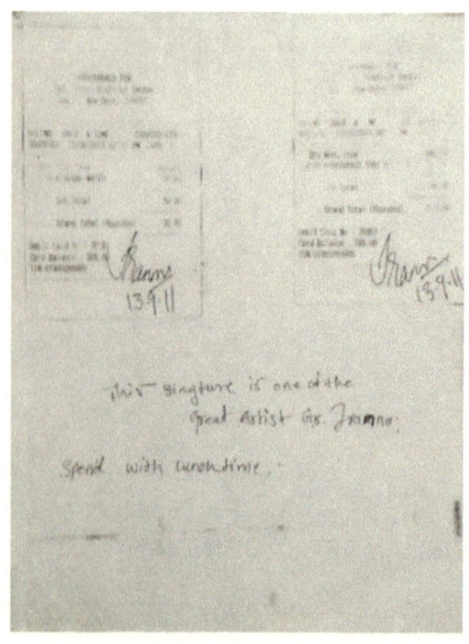

ARTIST G.R IRANNA FROM DHELI

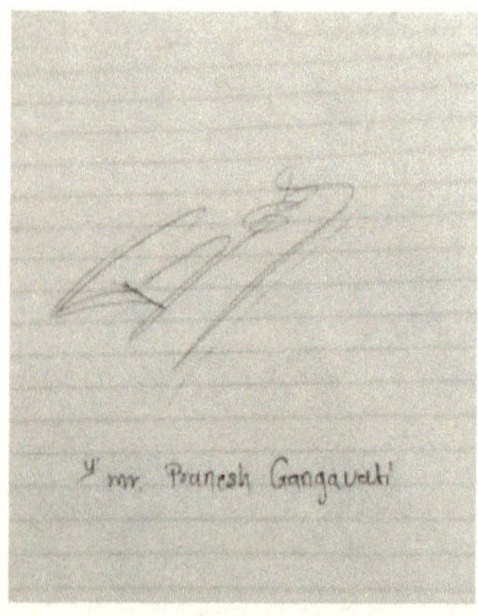

Actor and comedian Gangavati pranesh autograph

CHAPTER-15
WITH LEGEDND ARTIST MEMORY PHOTOES

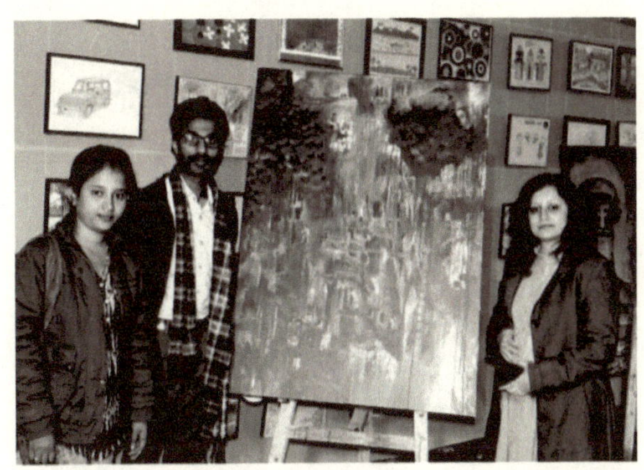

WITH ARTIST IN ODISSHA

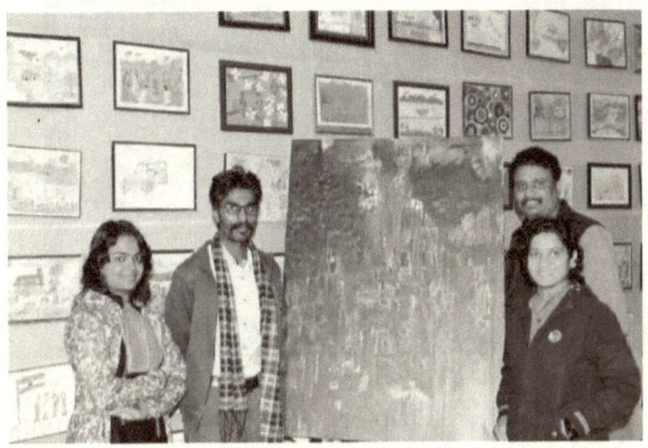

WITH ARTIST IN ODISSHA

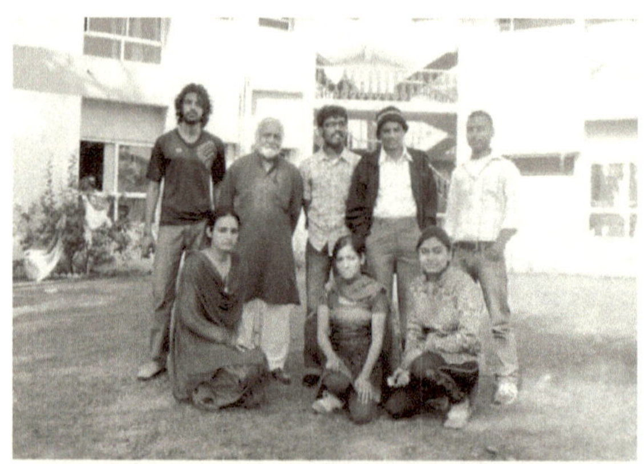

With hariyana arist national camp in Ujjain mp

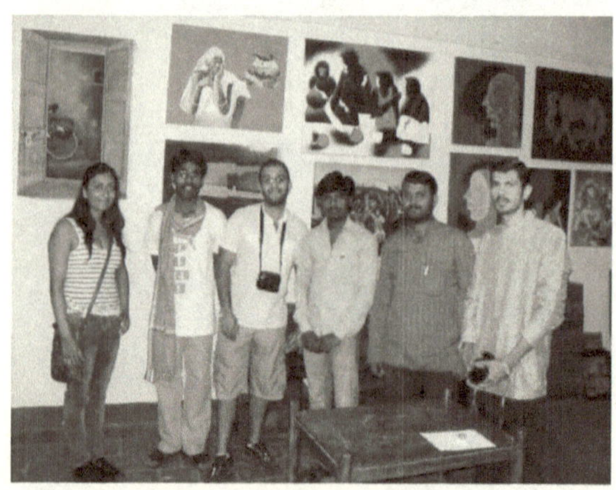

With German artist group exhibition in kerala

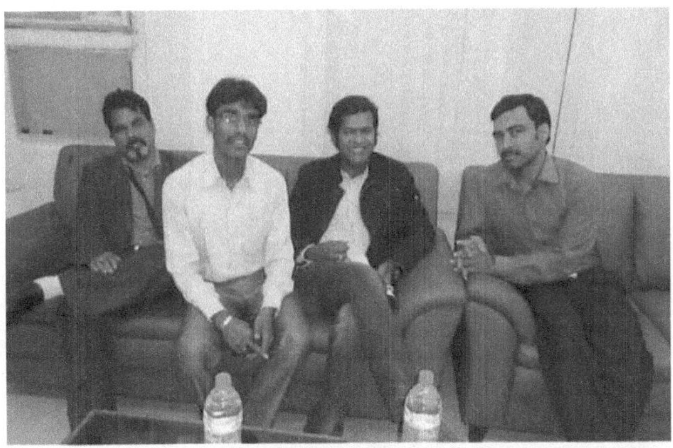

With international sand artist sudarshan patnayk odisha

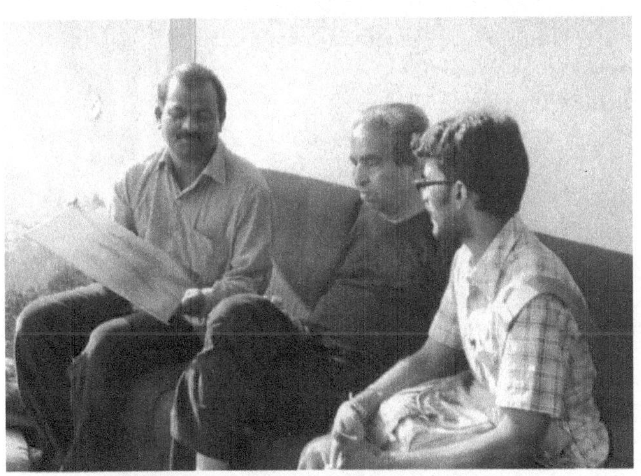

With artist shamshed Husain in Ujjain MP

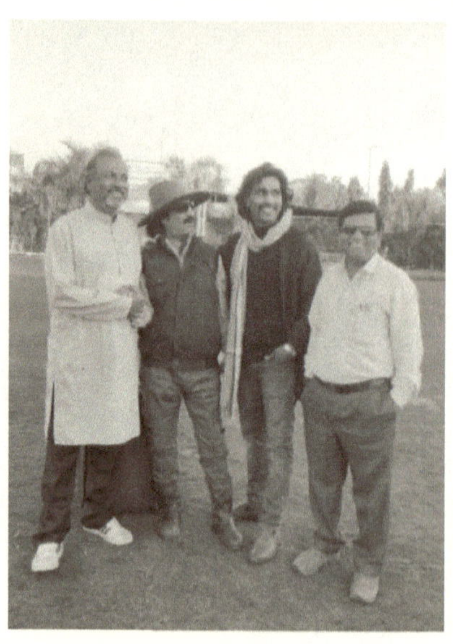

With artist Rajshekhar.s.
        Pawan and MD.makandar in rajastan

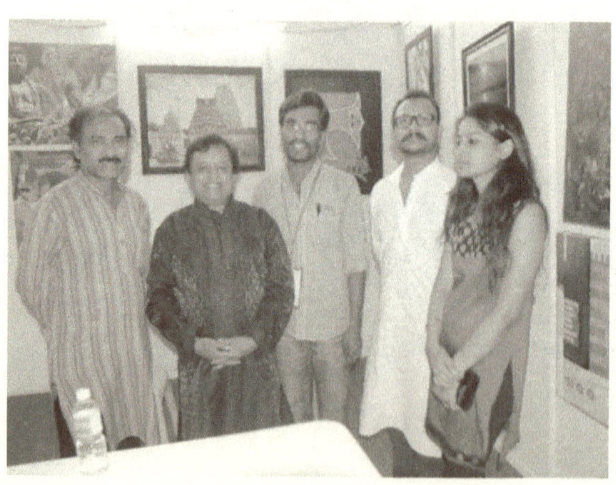

With Artist B k S varma and artist ayazuddin patel in benglore

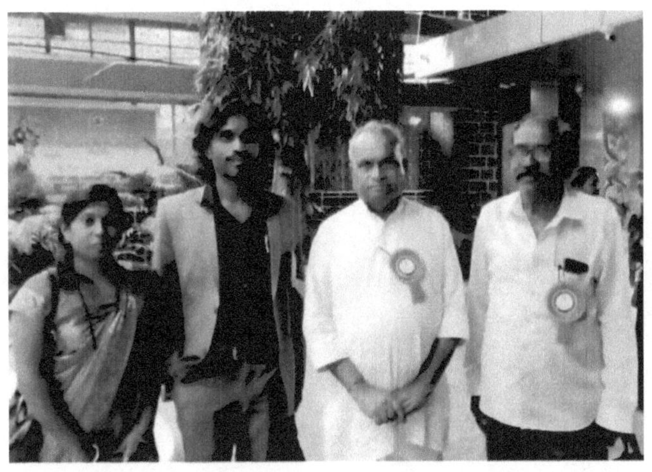

WITH MP BASAVARAJ SEDAM ,SINGER RAMESH JOSHI

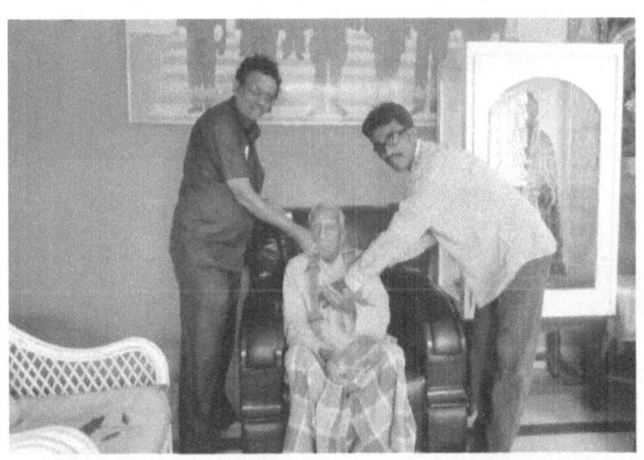

WITH FREEDOM FIGHTER SHREE VIDHYDAR GURUJI

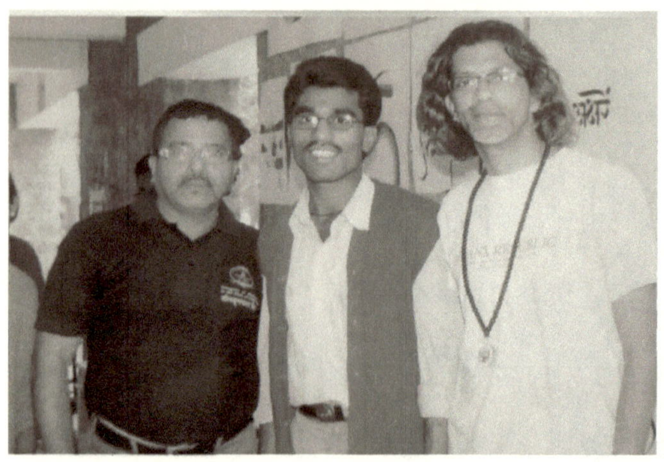

WITH CALLYGRAPHY ARTIST ACHYUT PALAV FROM MUMBAI

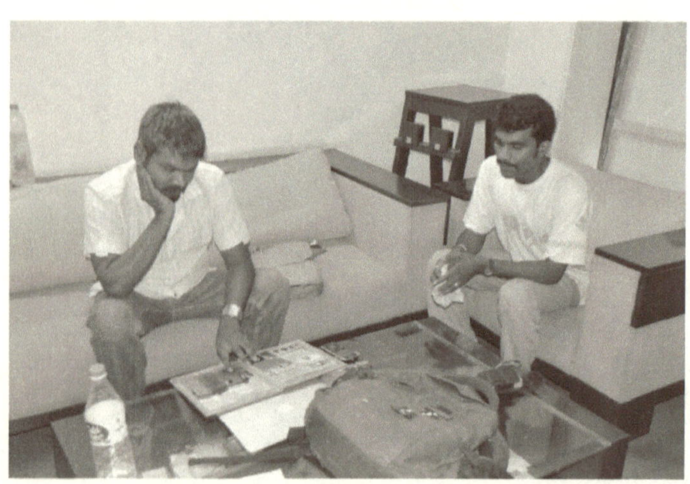

GREAT ARTIST GR IRANNA FROM DELHI

CHAPTER -16
ARTIST PAINTING AND DRAWING COLLECTION

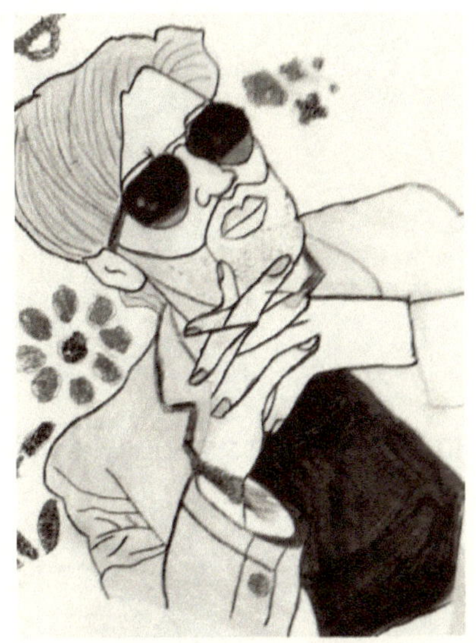

PORTRAIT BY STUDENT

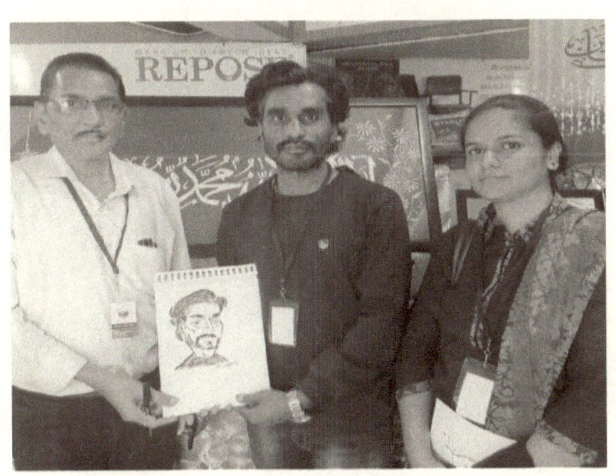

CARTOON PORTRAIT BY ARTIST M.SANJEEV

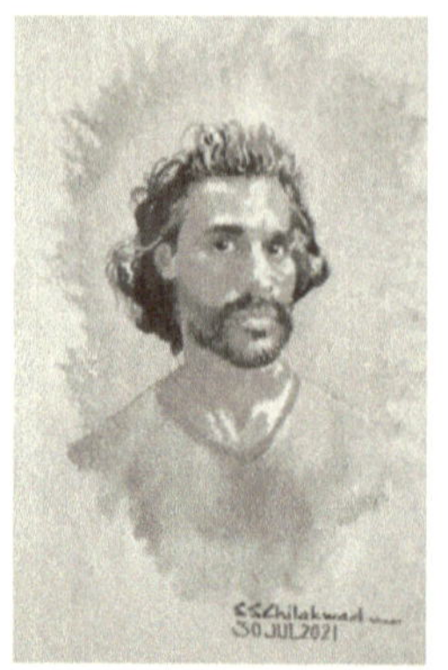

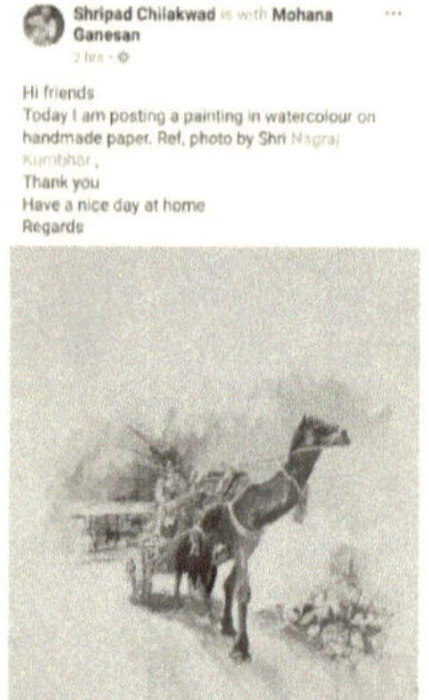

PORTRAIT BY ARTIST S.S CHILKWAD PUNE

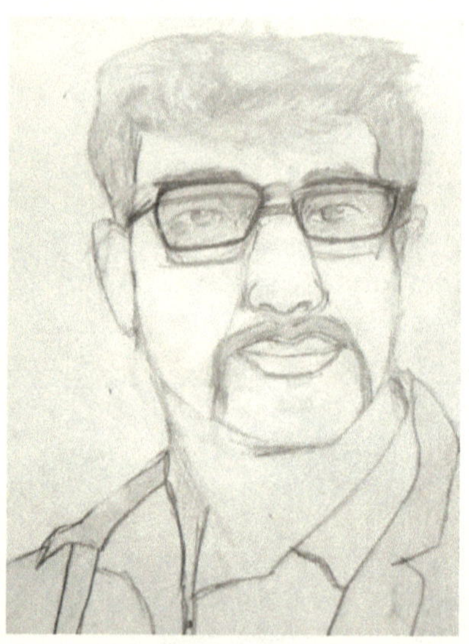

Nagraj   Portrait by student Prerana, benglore

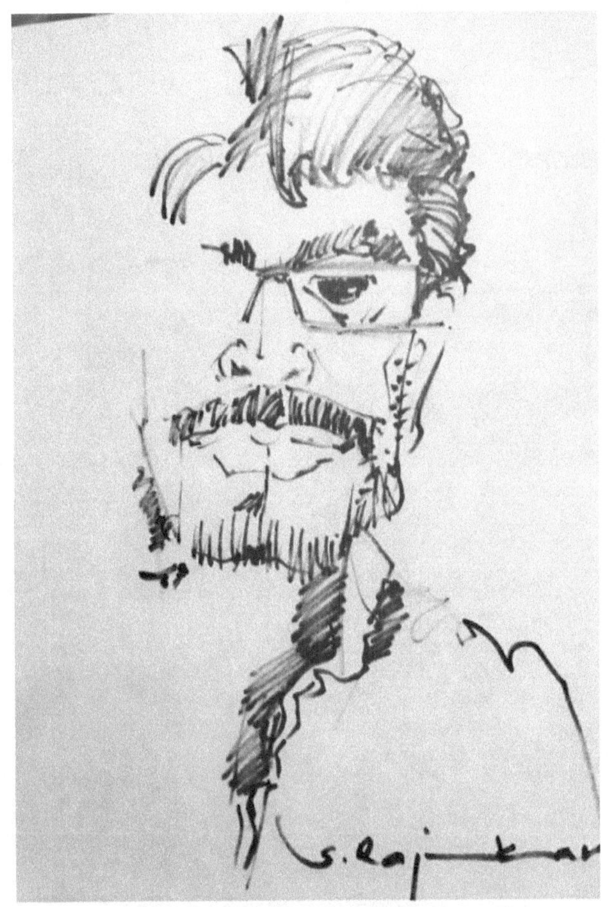

Portrait by Artist rajshekhar shamanna

CHAPTER -16
PUBLISHED PAPER CUTTING COLLECTION AND MEDIA

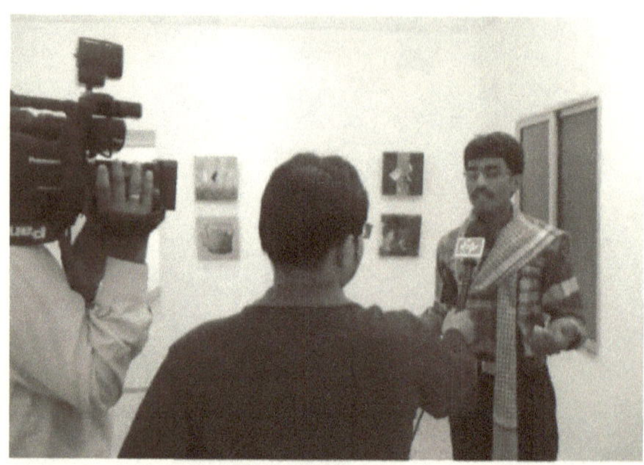

Interview by Odiya TV Channel in orissa

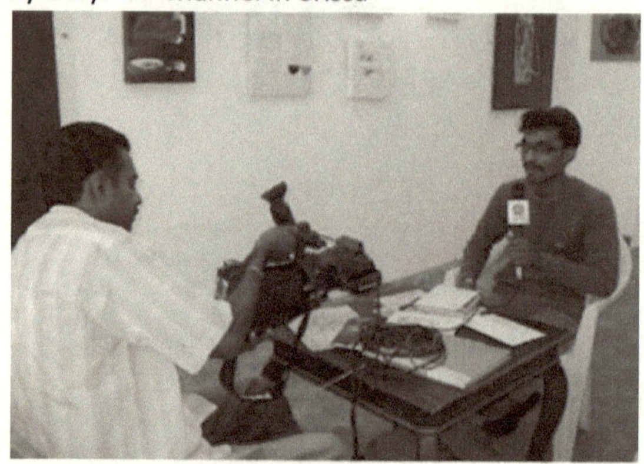

Interview by Malayalam manorama TV channel, in kerala

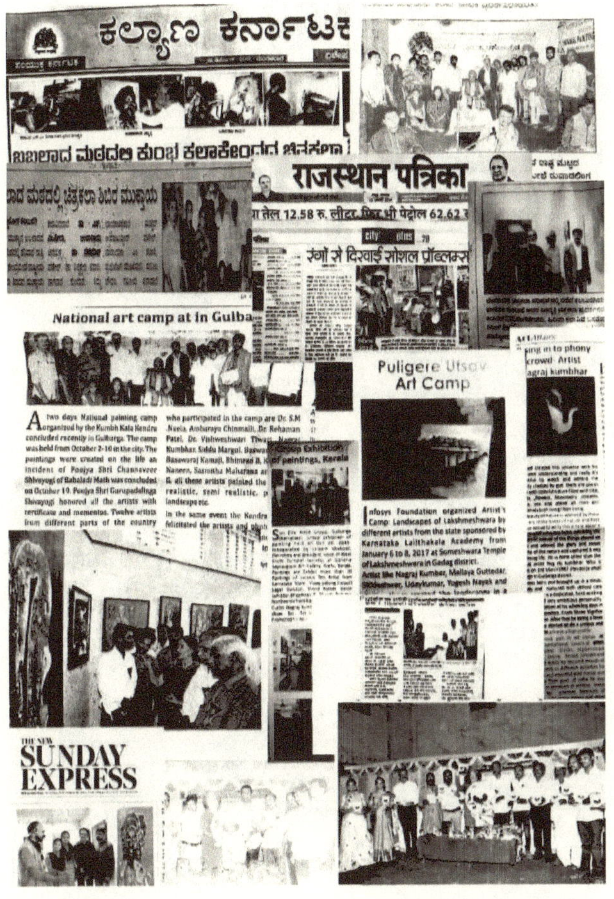

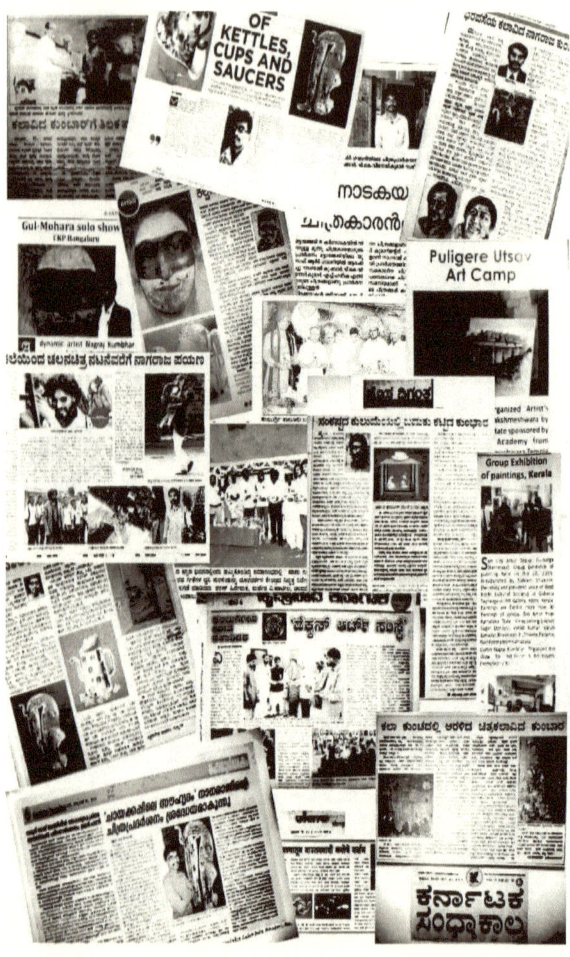

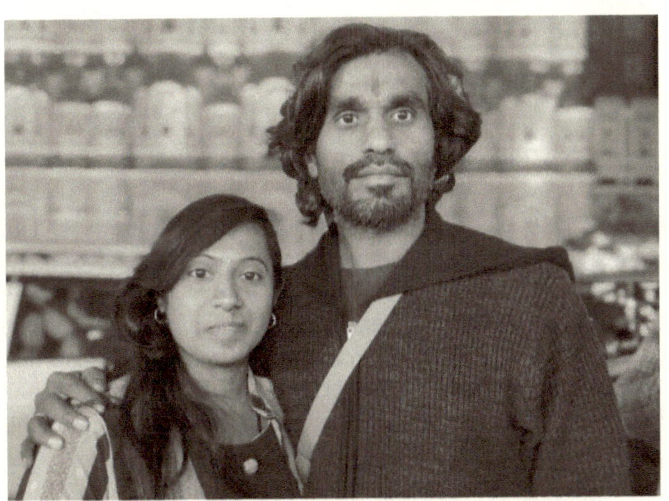

ARTIST NAGRAJ AND WIFE POOJA NAGRAJ

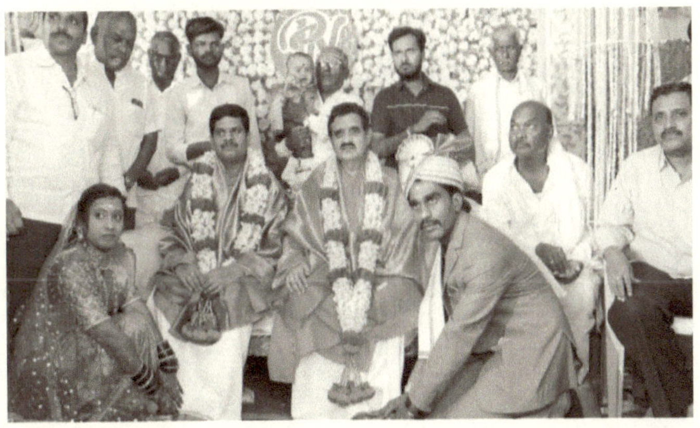

OPINION BY STUDENT.

ITS MY PLEASURE TO WRITE ABOUT NAGRAJ SIR .he works hard towards his goal.he is very creative artist..he opened eyes of many students .. Who only though artistis a person who not only do drawings but also he is multitasker.. .he identified and bought out the potentiality in student's .he introduced many of the art materials that many students of our age grow don't even know.i am really grateful to have in my life and very happy that I had been there during his work...

LOHIT R.

NK **an artist** biography

BIO-DATA
NAGRAJ R KUMBHAR
VISUAL ARTIST, WRITER, DIRECTOR AND ACTOR
BORN 03-03-1987, Heroor (B) Gulbarga
Academic Qualification:
Primary Education Jilha Shikshan Mandir Ozar Pune
High School Education Shri Vignahar vidhyalya Ozar Pune
PU College Education R.P. Sabnis Vidyamandir
Narayanagaon, Pune
Bachelor of Fine Arts (BFA) specialized in Painting from
Gulb.University, Gulb.
Master of Visual Arts (M.V.A.) Specialized in Painting, from, GUG.
AWARDS: --------
2022: Rashtriya kalaratna award by jaipur
2022:   national painting award in mount abuon the occasion of 75th
azadi ka amrit mahotsav by Bramhakumari's Rajasthan
2022: international art legend golden lotus award amalapuram
2016: "Ragvendrakala prashsti" by shri Gururagvendra
Sanskrutik akademi benglore
2013:   Best Art Teacher"International award, Orissa Modern
         Art Gallery, Bhubneshvar
2012   :"Eminent Educationist "Award, Delhi
2012   Lokmanya Tilak Award in painting at Pune
2011   : Gulbarga University Karnataka Rajyosthva Award inPainting
2011: Sahityaratna award by jind Narvana, Hariyana
SCHOLARSHIP---

2010 :   Youth Scholarship 2011-13 Govt. of India H.R.D New
Delhi
Member

Member: Suchitra film society banglore
Member   Film Writer Association, Mumbai
SOLOEXHIBITION--
--------2010   : Saynaugoun Art Gallery in Kochi;Kerala Sponsored by
         Karnataka Lalithakala Academy, Bangalor
2016   : Yusuf Art Gallery in Kochi; Kerala Sponsored by kannad

Mattu Sanskrut dept .karnataka.

2022   :   Bannada kudi solo exhibition of painting

GROUP   **EXHIBITIONS:**

2005 TO 09 Annual Day of Kalamahotsava
          M.M.K. College of visual arts,   Gulbarga

2009   :   Painting Group Exhibition, Chaitanyamayi Art Gallery, Gulbarga

2009   :   Deccan Art Society, Founder Members Art Exhibition, Gulbarga

2009   :   Painting Group Exhibition, Ankur Art Gallery, Gulbarga

2009   :   Mixed Bag Exhibition, In Venkatappa Art Gallery, Bangalore

2009   :   Mini Art Group Exhibition, Daira Gallery in Hyderabad

2011:   All India Drawing Group Exhibition in Bangalore

2011:   Sponsored by Panjab Lalitkala Academy Group
              Exhibition IChandigarh

2011   :   National Group Exhibition of Paintings in Kerla Kochin.

2013:   Group exhibition in Bhubaneswar, Orissa sponsored by Karnataka
          Kalalitkala Academy Bangalore

2012   :   Group show in Hyderabad Inspire Art Gallery.

2013:   (Chitra parise, Artfair Organized by Karnataka Lalith Akadami,Bnglore.

2010   : Art Society, Annual Art Exhibition Gulbarga.

2013:   Art Generation foundation Group, Exhibition of painting in
              coomar Swami hall mumbai.

2014:   winter show" Group exhibition of painting in suchitra art gallery,
          Mysore.

2015:   "Sun city artist" group exhibition of painting in kochi kerala.

2016   Group Exhibition of Painting in Jaipur Rajstan ,
              Sponserd by Karnataka lalit kala Academy Bangalore.

**PARTICIPATION   ART   COMPUTETION   AND
EXHIBITION**----------------------------------

2008:   Youth Festival Gangavati

2008:   22nd Lokamany Tilak Arts, Exhibition Pune

2008 :   Lalit Kala Academy selection, 38th Annual Art Exhibition,   Mangalore

<h1 style="text-align:center">NK an artist biography</h1>

2009 : Primer – Talent league art Exhibition, Mangalore

2009 : Gulbarga University Gulbarga Pratibha Mahotsava Art Exhibition Gulbarga

2009 : 23rd Lokmanya Tilak Art Exhibition Pune

2009 : Art & Culture National Exhibition, Gulbarga

2009 : Bidar Festival Art Exhibition

2010 : Pratibha Yuva Mahotsava Art Exhibition

2010 : Gulbarga University Gulbarga, Inter College Competition

2010: Kampu Painting Exhibition, in Gulbarga

2012 : 25th Silver Jubilee Lokmanya Tilak Art Exhibition Pune

2012 : Group photograph exhibition held in Chaitanyamayi Art Gallery

2022: national artist camp in mount abu rajasthan By brahmakumari's

2022: national artist camp in jaipur organized by rashtriya kala

Prava crayons jaipur rajasthan

PARTICIPITION   ARTIST   CAMP

2010: Alva's Varna Jagruthi State Art Camp In Modbidare

2010: Kalaparva (Ujjain) Student Artist Camp in the International

2013: The voice of canvas "Artist Camp organized by Orissa Modern Art Gallery in Bhubaneswar, Orissa state

2013: Artist camp April 15 'The World Art day" Artist camp In Gulbarga

2013: all India artist camp the "Doon valley public school Deovband, Sarangpur (up)

2015 National Art camp" KIRTI"EBES Engeering college Ghaziabad Delhi

2015 Gulbarga Artist Camp in Gulbarga, in by Gulbarga Academy of fine art, Gulbarga.

PARTICITATION ART WORKSHOP---

NK an artist biography

2005,2005,2006,2006,2007,2007: AnimationCamp ,Terracotta Camp,
Portrait Camp   Sculpture Camp, Traditional Camp, Calligraphy held
in M.M.K. College of
            visual   art Gulbarga
                2008:2ndNational Art Student Workshop CAVACollege
Mysore
            2009, 2009.2009, Graphic Workshop, Mural camp,
            In Cement, M.M.K. College of visual art Gulbarga.
            2010 : Creative Design Workshop M.M.K.College
                of Visual Art   Gulbarga.

COLLECTION:

Police Training Center Nagnahalli Gulbarga
Orissa Modern Art Gallery Bhubaneswar Orissa
M.M.K.College of Visual Art, Gulbarga
Eminent film singer Lata Mangeshkar, mumbai

ARTICALS   **ABOUT**
ME---

06Jun2008"   Ankur vedikeya, Aralida kalakusumagalu" Written by
S.R.Mannur.
12Dec2009   "DainikSamachar"Marathi"Nagrajacha Kunchlayahun
Vastvad Kaleeche   Darshan) Written by theGuraya Swami.
07 July 2009: Hosd Dingaht Kannada,"Sankastada Kulumeyalli
                BadukKattiddu Kumbhar) Written by Rabindra S
Deshmukh.
1 Aug 2010   : "Prajavani" Kannada newpaper,(Kumbharna
KalegaluVarna
            Vaividya) Written by Siddangouda.
1Aug2011   SamyuktaKarnataka,(SrujanshilMattPratibhavan
Kalavida
            Nagraj Written by Parashuram P.
5Jan2013:   published in Karnataka Sandyakal, daily Kannada news

            Paper, Written by Bhimashankar.
2012 Oct 30: Published in Raichurwani Kannada news
                Paper Artical byprof. Kiran patil
2016 march   "Barvsya klavida Nagraj Kumbhar"article published in
Samukt

NK an artist biography

Karnataka written by narayana Joshi.

2016   kumbars solo show at Kochi, ART AFFAIRS "article by
            DR.Raheman patel
2021   Chitrakaleinda chalan chitra kadege Nagraj payana by
            SamyuktaKarnataka written by revansidd hotti

Articles   about   me   Published   in   Book.
---Hyderabad   Karnataka   Kalavidar
Lalitkala   kosh"by   Gulbarga
University, Kannada and Cultural Dept.Karnataka.
Srujanshil   kalavida   Nagraj   Kumbhar   artical   published   in
"Drushyadhyan" Art Book Kaladarpan art book written by narayan
Joshi
**Published   Book   by
Me**---
1"Badukin Dariyalli Preeti" Kannada poem book published in,
2009.2010.
2"Nammur shri hullikantishvar pavadgalu"Research book Kannada
published in
2016
3 Babladiya pavada purusha shri chennaveera shivayogi charitra
darshan
4 taych watevarti punha ekda Marathi novel Witten by Nagraj
5 shevadsa pan Marathi book written by Nagraj
6 kuch yaade Hindi shahari book
7 bannada belakindi art book
8 kalayana Marathi book
9 halabanadastu holeyuva kalavida Kannada book
10 kavyanjali Marathi poem book
11 kale mimanse art book
12 daiva sakshatkar mattu pavada
13 kalpavruksha G M Chandrashekar
14 kumbhakala Kendra smarana sanchike
15 once again on the same path book translated in English
UPCOMING   BOOKS

MANNINA MADKEYA MIMMANSE......ART KANNADA BOOK
PAGE 14 HINDI NOVELS

PAGE 14 NOVELS IN ENGLISH
NK …ARTIST NAGRAJ KUMBHAR IN ENGLISH

ARTICLES BY ME--

29 July2010:   Kale beleyuvudu hege"Vegavahini" Kannada dina Patrike

1Aug 2010:   Kalavidana Badukeena olanota- Rajshekhar"Vegavahini Kannada Dina Patrike,4 Aug 2009:   Art, Nature relation with Life "Kranti Paper"

9 Aug 2010: Kalavidana Chintaneyalli Mudid rekha chitragluPrakash Gadkar,"Vegavahini" Kannada Dina Patrike,22Aug 2010: Kalavidana Kale Ballavaru yaruVegavahini" Kannada Dina Patrike,28 Aug 2010: Shrujana sheel Kalavida – Gautam v.Andani"Vegavahini"Kannada Dina Patrike,4 Sep 2010 : Prkruti, Kale

  mattu jivanakku Bidalarada Nantu"Vegavahini"Kannada   Dina Patrike,11Sep201   : Chayachitra kalavide Smeeta Bhattvara

Kiru nota"Vegavahini Kannada Dina Patrike,15 Sep 2010:   Yuva Kalavidaralli

Agraganya KalavidaRamgiri Police PatilVegavahini"Kannada Dina Patrike

Jully2013   "Kale inda Makkala Manovikasa Mattu Sruzanshil' published in Kannada news paper.

MURAL WORKSHOP

: Mural Paintings in Deviratan resort at Jaipur (Rajasthan).

: Mural paintings in Diamond Hotel in Lucknow (UP).

: Mural Paintings International school in Allahabad (UP).

PROJECT   WORK   AND   DOCUMENTRY FILM---

2o13 Gram charitre khosh" project work of folk art .Child creative art documentary movie.heroor b village shri hulikanthishvar gudi darshan "idu satya, Documentary movie published in udaya TV Chanel.

2021   Nadapriyana Nadayaana Documentary films, about singer Ramesh Joshi

ACTED IN UPCOMING MOVIES --

Ganapati bappa morya Kannada film directed by Anand vathar

Chargsheet film directed by gururaj kulakarni, Ninagaagi-2 Kannada film directed

 by prakash nayak, Sangeetmaya film

STORY WRITTEN AND ACTING IN SHORT FILMS----
"QUEEN" father and daughter emotional story directed by anand vathar
THE LAST PAINTING….short film in Hindi
First letter …Emotional love story…
Magalalli kanda taytana...Father and Daughter emotional story
SHORT FILMS DIRECTED BY ME---------------------------------
PAPER BOAT …ART FILMS, PAGE-1...SHORT FILM, GAVIGUDI IN LAND LETTER,
   BADIGE MANE, and MODALA NOTA, TANMEYA...KAALUDAARI, NEERIKSHE, BRAHME.BLACK PEN, 12 MOUNA…KANNADA WEBSERIS
VEDIO ALBUM SONG--
1 JAI SHRI GANESHA, 2 MUNDENU VEDIO SONG
3 SHIVATANDAV STROTRAM ….KANNADA RIMIX SONG
4 NE KRISHNA BEGANE BAARO...KANNADA RIMIX SONG
5 JAROORI THHA HINDI VEDIO RIMIX SONG
AUDIO ALBUM SONG AND CD RELEASING----------------
Haadu nannadu dhwani nimmadu KANNADA AUDIO CD
Jai shri ganesha Kannada audio album song IN KANNADA
Appu ni baro marali audio song IN KANNADA
Jai shri ganesha Kannada audio album song IN MARATHI

RESIDENCE IN GULBARAGA ------------------------------

NAGRAJ R KUMBHAR
Mobile: +9164033602, 9483834208
E-mail: NagrajKumbhar@gmail.com

NK an artist biography